£2-50
37

Office of Strategic Services 1942–45

The World War II Origins of the CIA

EUGENE LIPTAK

ILLUSTRATED BY RICHARD HOOK
Consultant editor Martin Windrow

First published in Great Britain in 2009 by Osprey Publishing,
Midland House, West Way, Botley, Oxford OX2 0PH, UK
443 Park Avenue South, New York, NY 10016, USA
Email: info@ospreypublishing.com

Print ISBN: 978 184603 463 3
ebook ISBN: 978 1 84908 098 9

Editor: Martin Windrow
Design: Ken Vail Graphic Design, Cambridge, UK (kvgd.com)
Typeset in Sabon and Myriad Pro
Index by Fineline Editorial Services
Originated by PPS Grasmere Ltd, Leeds, UK
Printed in China through World Print Ltd.

09 10 9 8 7 6 5 4 3 2 1

A CIP catalog record for this book is available from the British Library

FOR A CATALOG OF ALL BOOKS PUBLISHED BY OSPREY MILITARY
AND AVIATION PLEASE CONTACT:

Osprey Direct, c/o Random House Distribution Center,
400 Hahn Road, Westminster, MD 21157
Email: uscustomerservice@ospreypublishing.com

Osprey Direct, The Book Service Ltd, Distribution Centre,
Colchester Road, Frating Green, Colchester, Essex, CO7 7DW
E-mail: customerservice@ospreypublishing.com

www.ospreypublishing.com

DEDICATION

This book is dedicated with love and respect to Dr William S. Augat

ACKNOWLEDGEMENTS

The author is grateful to the following individuals and institutions that
helped make this book possible: Jeff Bass, Rene Defourneaux, Thomas L.
Ensminger, Herb Friedman, Jim Gray, Ian Grimwood, Alyce Guthrie of the
WWII PT Boats Museum and Archives in Germantown, TN; Ron Hairston, Les
Hughes, Lawrence H. McDonald, Patrick K. O'Donnell, Judith Pearson,
Gordon Rottman, Edward Schmitt, Ronald Volstad, Thomas Wheeler, and
the staff at the National Archives in College Park, MD; the JFK Special
Warfare Museum at Ft Bragg, NC; and the US Army Military History Institute
in Carlisle, PA.

ARTIST'S NOTE

Readers may care to note that the original paintings from which the
colour plates in this book were prepared are available for private sale.
All reproduction copyright whatsoever is retained by the Publishers. All
enquiries should be addressed to:

Richard Hook, PO Box 475, Hailsham, East Sussex BN27 2SL, UK

The Publishers regret that they can enter into no correspondence upon
this matter.

ABBREVIATIONS USED IN THIS TEXT:

ACRU	Air Crew Rescue Unit
AGFRTS	Air and Ground Forces Resources and Technical Staff
BIS	Bureau of Investigation and Statistics (Chinese)
CIC	Counter-Intelligence Corps
CID	Central Information Division
COI	Coordinator of Information
EOU	Enemy Objectives Unit
FBI	Federal Bureau of Investigation
FIS	Foreign Information Service
G-2	Army Intelligence
G-3	Army Operations
JCS	Joint Chiefs of Staff
LARU	Lambertsen Amphibious Respiratory Unit
MD	Map Division
MO	Morale Operations
MU	Maritime Unit
OG	Operational Group
OWI	Office of War Information
PWE	Political Warfare Executive (British)
R&A	Research and Analysis
R&D	Research & Development
SACO	Sino-American Cooperative Organization
SAS	Special Air Service (British)
SCI	Special Counter Intelligence
SD	Special Duty (British)
SF	Special Force
SFHQ	Special Force Headquarters
SI	Secret Intelligence
SIS	Secret Intelligence Service (British)
SO	Special Operations
SOE	Special Operations Executive (British)
SOU	Ship Observer Unit
UDT	Underwater Demolition Team

CONTENTS

OFFICE OF STRATEGIC SERVICES 1942–45

INTRODUCTION

In July 1940, William J. Donovan was sent to Great Britain by the Roosevelt administration to determine if the island nation had the ability to fight on after the German victories in Western Europe during May and June. Donovan, a Medal of Honor holder from World War I and a successful Wall Street lawyer, met with Britain's leadership, toured her defenses, and was given access to her clandestine services – the SIS and the newly created SOE. After delivering a report calling for increased American aid to Britain, Donovan advocated the creation of an American centralized intelligence service to combat enemy espionage and subversion, which was believed at that time to be a major factor in the fall of France. On July 11, 1941, by order of President Roosevelt, the Coordinator of Information (COI) was established as a civilian agency with Donovan as its director. Its mission was to gather and analyze security information obtained from agents around the world and from government departments and agencies. COI was to report its findings to President Roosevelt and to government agencies as he deemed appropriate. The FBI and the military services mistrusted this new intelligence agency, which they believed could threaten their control over American intelligence-gathering.

Donovan first established the Foreign Information Service branch under the direction of playwright Robert E. Sherwood, to prepare and distribute "white" or

Shown here visiting Detachment 404 headquarters in Ceylon in July 1945, Gen William J. Donovan was the sole director of the OSS during its brief existence. Regarded as the forefather of the Central Intelligence Agency, Donovan also has the unique achievement of being the first recipient of all four of the highest American decorations that can be bestowed: the Congressional Medal of Honor, the Distinguished Service Cross, the Distinguished Service Medal, and the National Security Medal.

factual propaganda across Europe and the Pacific by radio, print and film. The Research & Analysis branch was created next, to evaluate information obtained by COI and distribute reports based on its findings. Other founding branches included the Foreign Nationalities branch, to interview arriving foreign immigrants; the Field Photography Division; and a Special Activities section for spying, sabotage and guerrilla warfare. After observing the damaging rivalry between Britain's separate SIS and SOE over the demarkation of responsibilities, Donovan decided to split Special Activities into a Secret Intelligence branch for intelligence-gathering, and a Special Operations branch for subversive operations, with the goal of better coordination with the respective British agencies while still operating under a single clandestine organization. Since COI was still getting itself established and directing its efforts towards Europe, it was not involved in the intelligence failure that preceded the attack on Pearl Harbor in December 1941.

With America now in the war, Donovan realized that unconventional warfare conducted by COI needed support from the newly established Joint Chiefs of Staff. Sherwood was concerned that putting COI under military control would hinder the ability of the civilian-staffed FIS to operate effectively. By contrast, Donovan believed that both "white" and "black" propaganda (designed to subvert the target audience by any devious means possible) were best employed under the direction of the military.

President Roosevelt settled the issue by signing Executive Order 9128 on June 13, 1942; this removed FIS from COI and placed it under the new Office of War Information. What was left of COI became the Office of Strategic Services under the jurisdiction of the JCS. The JCS gave the OSS equal status with the other military services and authorized it to gather intelligence and conduct subversive activities and psychological warfare. The OSS was not allowed to decode enemy communications, or to conduct intelligence operations in the United States and South America, which was the FBI's responsibility. While the OSS would be active in the China-Burma-India Theater, despite his efforts Donovan could not convince either Gen Douglas MacArthur or Adm Chester Nimitz to allow the OSS to operate in the Pacific Theater.)

* * *

Only weeks after the end of the war President Harry Truman signed Executive Order 9621 disbanding the OSS, effective 1 October 1945. With the exception of R&A transferring to the State Department, and SI and X-2 Counterespionage to the War Department, the OSS ceased to exist.

As the Cold War became a reality, the need for a centralized intelligence service reasserted itself. In September 1947 Truman signed the National Security Act that established the Central Intelligence Agency; many OSS veterans joined the CIA, including four future directors. Others stayed in the military, and used their OSS experience to make American special operations forces the elite fighting units they are today.

ORGANIZATION

From the 1,000 staff that remained after FIS was transferred to OWI in June 1942, the OSS expanded to a peak of over 13,000 personnel by late 1944, and at least 24,000 people worked for the OSS at one time or another during its brief existence. Members from all the military branches served in the OSS, and it provided the USMC its few opportunities to engage in operations against the

Morale Operations branch broadcast popular songs of the day with German lyrics to keep its target audience tuned in for the "black" propaganda that followed; a **total of 312 of these songs were recorded in New York and flown to London to be broadcast between July 1944 and April 1945. The** musicians and singers hired to perform these songs in German were unaware they were working for the OSS. (NARA)

Germans. Civilian staff worked as clerks, analysts, scientists, engineers, and even behind enemy lines. About 4,000 women worked for the OSS either as civilians or in uniform, performing clerical roles and helping prepare missions in operational theaters, and some – such as Virginia Hall, and locally recruited agents like Hélène Deschamps – operated behind enemy lines. The OSS was organized into the following branches.

SECRET INTELLIGENCE

The SI branch gathered and reported military intelligence from operational areas by unorthodox means, to include: the location, movement and patterns of activity of enemy units; the strength and capabilities of resistance movements; the location of infrastructure and industrial targets; and the gathering of economic, political, social and psychological intelligence. This was accomplished by positioning agents in enemy territory, acting in direct liaison with resistance groups, and obtaining tactical intelligence for Allied troops near the front lines. SI established its Technical Section to review and distribute agent reports pertaining to the German secret weapons program, and supplied over 2,000 reports on German atomic research to the Manhattan Project. As well as initiating their own operations, SI fulfilled specific requests from the military services, and also obtained reports from the clandestine services of Allied nations.

SI was divided into four Geographic Desks that coordinated operations in Europe, Africa, the Middle East and the Far East, each being subdivided into sections devoted to specific countries. While most SI operations originated from the Geographic Desks in Washington, control was exercised by overseas field bases for better coordination and response to local situations. Washington did maintain direct control over SI operations in neutral nations, where the primary focus was on infiltrating agents into and obtaining intelligence from bordering enemy-occupied countries.

SI had difficulty finding enough experienced personnel not only to operate behind enemy lines, but also to staff the coordinating field bases. Consequently, many Americans who were recruited as agents in fact became operations officers (handlers) because of their language skills and knowledge of the local culture, while agents to actually operate in enemy territory were recruited from local populations. SI agents reported their findings to their SI handlers either by portable radios, through couriers, or in person if they exfiltrated back through enemy lines.

Within SI, a **Labor Section** obtained industrial intelligence and recruited agents through the labor unions and organizations in different countries. The **Ship Observer Unit,** established in December 1942, gathered shipping intelligence from seamen's organizations and from sailors who had recently sailed from ports in neutral or enemy-held countries or in Germany itself. Informal interviews with – or actual agent recruitment among – seamen of neutral merchant fleets yielded information on harbor installations, naval bases, cargoes, and the current situation in occupied territories. Sailors recruited by SOU also obtained foreign publications, and helped infiltrate OSS agents into enemy territory.

SPECIAL OPERATIONS

The SO branch was created to take the war directly to the enemy through unorthodox warfare – the direct sabotage of enemy targets, and training local resistance forces in guerrilla warfare. Small SO teams or circuits sabotaged targets of strategic importance such as factories or railway tunnels, or targets of a tactical nature like bridges and supply dumps. SO teams organized, supplied and trained local resistance groups with Allied weaponry, to conduct a sustained insurgency campaign of sabotage and ambush. Since many of these activities were in direct support of Allied operations, SO units came under the authority of their respective Allied theater commanders. Several sections of SO – such as the Operational Groups, Maritime Unit, and Technical Development – later became separate OSS branches in their own right.

Operational Groups

Established as a separate branch from SO in May 1943, OG conducted irregular warfare directly against enemy forces – raiding installations, ambushing supply lines, occupying key infrastructure to prevent its destruction, as well as supplying, training, and operating alongside resistance groups. In contrast to other OSS operatives behind the lines, OG always fought in military uniform. Uniquely, OG were formed exclusively with first-

This leaflet from "The League of Lonely German Women" instructs any German soldier that if he cuts out the heart symbol and displays it while on home leave he could soon enjoy the intimate attentions of a German girl who is missing her man. Private Barbara Lauwers of OSS Morale Operations came up with this idea after being told by a German POW that the most disturbing news that a soldier could receive from home was that his wife or girlfriend was seeing another man. Many German soldiers were later captured in possession of League leaflets and pins. (Courtesy Herb Friedman)

Sommer 1944.

Lieber Frontsoldat!
Wann kommst Du wieder auf Urlaub?

Wann wirst Du Deine harten Soldatenpflichten wieder einmal vergessen können, wenigstens für ein paar Tage voll Freude, Glück und Liebe? Wir in der Heimat wissen von Deinem heldenhaften Kampf, wir verstehen aber, dass auch der Tapferste einmal müde wird und ein so feines Kissen, Zärtlichkeit und gesundes Vergnügen braucht.

WIR WARTEN AUF DICH:

auf Dich, der in einer fremden Stadt allein seinen Urlaub verbringen muss; auf Dich, dem der Krieg sein Heim genommen hat; auf Dich, der ohne Frau, Braut oder Flirt in der Welt steht.

WIR WARTEN AUF DICH:

schneide unser Abzeichen aus diesem Briefe aus. In jedem Kaffee, in jeder Bar in der Nähe eines Bahnhofs, lehne es sichtbar an Dein Glas; gar bald wird sich ein Mitglied unseres V.E.K. Deiner annehmen, und Deine Frontträume und die Sehnsucht einsamer Nächte werden Erfüllung finden... Wir wollen Dich, nicht Dein Geld, darum lass Dir stets unsere Mitgliedskarte vorher zeigen. Mitglieder gibt es überall, da wir deutsche Frauen unsere Pflichten zur Heimat und ihren Verteidigern verstanden haben.

Natürlich sind wir auch selbstsüchtig. — jahrelang von unseren Männern getrennt, mit all den Fremden um uns herum, möchten wir wieder einmal einen richtigen deutschen Jungen an's Herz drücken. Nur keine Hemmungen: Deine Frau, Schwester oder Geliebte ist auch eine der unseren.

Wir denken an Dich und auch an Deutschlands Zukunft. Was rastet — rostet...

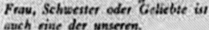

VEREIN EINSAMER KRIEGERFRAUEN

or second-generation Americans of Norwegian, Greek, Italian, Yugoslavian, Polish, German or French heritage. Recruited from US Army infantry and airborne units, each OG had at least several members who could speak the local language fluently. From August 1944, OGs in Europe were collectively identified as 2671st Special Reconnaissance Battalion (Provisional), which would be awarded the Presidential Unit Citation; Detachment 101 in Burma was the only other OSS unit to be so honored.

(For Special Force Detachments, see below under "France and the Low Countries.")

Maritime Unit

The MU separated from SO in June 1943. Its purpose was to use the sea to place OSS operatives behind enemy lines, supply resistance movements, conduct shoreline reconnaissance and sabotage maritime targets. Because of this unique mission, MU developed its own special equipment independently of the Research & Development branch.

MORALE OPERATIONS

This branch was established in January 1943, to cause disharmony and chaos among enemy troops and civilians by the use of "black" propaganda – lies and deception, spread by radio broadcasts and printed materials – to subvert enemy morale. A key distinction between OWI and MO propaganda was its perceived origins: OWI material was overtly advertised as coming directly from the Allies, but MO material was crafted to give the impression that it came from resistance movements or from the enemy itself. Although the direct impact of such methods is difficult to quantify precisely, countermeasures such as denials in official publications and the jamming of radio broadcasts proved that MO activities did not go unnoticed. Several instances were noted of rumors and lies that MO had spread behind enemy lines turning up later in Allied reports or the press.

Radio broadcasts

MO transmitted its "black" radio programs into the Reich from stations around its periphery. The first originated from Tunisia in June 1943; broadcast into Italy, it was called *Italo Balbo* after the late Italian air marshal. To create divisions between Italians and Germans it played on Italian suspicions that his death in 1940 was connected with his opposition to Italy's ties with Germany, and called for popular action against the Fascist regime. *Italo Balbo* ceased after the invasion of Sicily. Another MO station code-named *Boston* was established in Izmir, Turkey, to target German forces in the Balkans with news of military reverses and events on the German home front. It operated from August to October 1944, when several direct acts of sabotage forced its closure.

One of the most successful black radio programs was a joint effort with Britain's PWE called *Soldatensender-Calais*, which began broadcasting to German forces in July 1944. Masquerading as a German radio station from that still-occupied French port (and renamed *Soldatensender-West* after Calais' liberation in September 1944), its programs actually originated from Milton Bryant in England. To maintain a captive audience for its subversive messages *Soldatensender* played popular American songs that were composed, sung and recorded in German by artists such as Marlene Dietrich. After the July 1944 assassination attempt on Hitler, *Soldatensender* broadcast the names of alleged conspirators involved in the plot so that the Gestapo would disrupt the German leadership by pursuing these leads. The US Twelfth Army Group reported that 90 percent of German POWs taken in the summer of 1944 admitted to listening to this station.

As Allied armies reached the German border MO began to broadcast directly into Germany from stations on the continent. Programs such as *Westdeutscher Volkssender* and *Volkssender Drei* conjured up fictitious resistance groups within Germany, calling for a popular revolt against the Nazis. MO recruited German POWs to record broadcasts, including a major whose voice resembled that of Gen Ludwig Beck, the former Chief of General Staff who committed suicide after being implicated in the July 1944 attempt

Five members of OG Team "Donald" beside the "Carpetbagger" B-24 that will drop them over Brittany in August 1944. They wear the British X-type parachute routinely used for clandestine night drops; being a "canopy last" design this did not open until the jumper had dropped clear of the slipstream (see Plate A1). The low altitude of the jump made reserve parachutes pointless, so fully loaded M1936 field bags are worn in their place. OSS personnel who successfully completed British parachute training were entitled to wear British parachute wings; the man on the far left displays them below his SF wings. (NARA)

on Hitler's life. The convincingly impersonated "Beck" blamed Hitler for losing the war and called for an end to the Nazi regime if Germany was to survive. The Nazis' sensitivity was indicated by their very diligent jamming of further broadcasts from "General Beck."

One technological advantage that MO and PWE exploited in January–April 1945 was a 600,000-watt Aspidistra transmitter in Woburn, England; this overpowered and interrupted German radio broadcasts with false news bulletins, anti-Nazi rhetoric and rebuttal of key points from the program that was being interrupted. The enemy could not jam these interruptions without blocking their own programs sharing the same frequency. When the Allies crossed into Germany, MO black radio announced false Allied movements and German defeats to confuse the Wehrmacht and reinforce the sentiment that further resistance was futile. MO

A — SECRET INTELLIGENCE

1: SI AGENT; HARRINGTON AIRFIELD, NORTHAMPTONSHIRE, ENGLAND, SPRING 1944

OSS agents who jumped into occupied territory wore British one-piece canvas "striptease suits" to protect their clothing from telltale dirt or damage during a parachute drop. Produced in at least three slightly differing models, hooded and unhooded, they were made from unlined camouflage material and occasionally in white for snowy terrain. The suits had two front zippers from the neck to the foot for quick removal. Many internal and external press-stud pockets accomodated an entrenching tool to bury the suit and parachute upon landing, a pistol, claspknife and fighting knife, a first aid kit, torch and other small accessories, and a large dorsal pocket held a cushioning pad or a small valise. Lace-on knee pads were sometimes used, as were overboots in brown or blue, and leather gauntlets. The jump helmet was made of sponge rubber and covered with the same camouflage material; it had a buckle-over chin-cup and press studs to attach an oxygen mask when necessary. This agent is wearing the standard British "X-type" parachute.

2: SPECIAL FORCE DETACHMENT; HQ US SEVENTH ARMY, SOUTHERN FRANCE, SUMMER 1944

The OSS did not have its own unique uniforms or insignia during the war. Its military personnel wore standard uniforms and insignia, depending on the service from which they were recruited, in order to stay as inconspicuous as possible. This OSS officer is wearing standard M1 helmet, olive drab wool shirt and trousers and double-buckle boots, and his insignia is limited to a national brassard and the 7th Army patch. His weapons are a 9mm UD-42 Marlin submachine gun and a holstered Colt M1911A1 pistol.

3: SI AGENT; ITALY, SUMMER 1944

The HiStandard .22cal silenced pistol was the most useful of the special weapons developed for the OSS. There are no known wartime photographs of it being used in the field; this reconstruction is based on a July 1944 R&D report from the Mediterranean, which stated that SI agents found the pistol effective when sniping from windows at short range.

1

2

3

MO branch fabricated *Das Neue Deutschland*, purportedly the newspaper of an anti-Nazi peace party inside Germany. Resistance groups were given copies to be distributed where the German troops in their areas would find them. (Courtesy Herb Friedman)

also sent coded messages to fictitious resistance groups in Germany, with instructions to cross out letters of the Nazi party initials "NSDAP" on public display so only the N and the D remained; Allied troops found examples of this on posters and official party signs in the towns they passed through.

In the Far East, MO established a radio station near Chittagong, India, north of the Burmese border, to imitate the Thai-language Radio Tokyo broadcasts in Thailand. To increase plausibility the station broadcast near the same frequency and immediately before the regularly scheduled airtime of Radio Tokyo. Thai agents were used to announce news about Japanese battlefield setbacks, and this material was even printed subsequently in Thai newspapers, since they were required to print what Radio Tokyo reported. Even after the Japanese compelled the Thai government to reveal that the MO broadcasts were phony they remained popular with Thai listeners. MO also established a radio station in Kunming, China, which was heard in the coastal areas occupied by the Japanese; these broadcasts encouraged nonviolent resistance and sent messages to fictitious Chinese guerrilla groups. One program based on a Chinese fortune-teller predicted that a major (albeit unspecified) disaster would directly hit Japan in early August 1945.

MO was also able to broadcast directly into the Japanese home islands, recruiting Nissei and Issei personnel to help produce the *Voice of the People* program in San Francisco; a Japanese POW was used to ensure that colloquial expressions in the broadcasts were contemporary for Japanese ears. These programs were recorded on disks and flown to Saipan, where, from April 1945 until the war's end, they were broadcast into Japan from an OWI transmitter. Ostensibly originating from Japan itself, these programs emphasized Japan's inevitable defeat, demanded an end to the war, and called on the populace to drive the militarists from power. Except for the first and last two transmissions, however, the Japanese successfully jammed all 124 broadcasts.

Printed materials
Morale Operations also produced printed materials to undermine enemy civilian and military morale, such as leaflets, false newspapers, documents, death notices

MO's "black" propaganda materials were printed close to or in the operational area where they were to be distributed, in order to keep them convincingly relevant for the intended readers. Press X was a portable printing press developed for MO personnel who did not have access to local conventional presses. (Author's photograph)

and poison pen letters. Leaflets were either air-dropped over a large area of territory or distributed by locally recruited agents; MO also provided resistance groups with materials so that they could produce leaflets on their own. In spring 1945 MO initiated Operation "Cornflakes," where planes from the US Army Fifteenth Air Force attacked trains carrying German mail and simultaneously dropped mailbags full of MO material nearby; these were recovered during the clean-up, and their contents were mailed throughout the Reich.

The attempted assassination of Hitler in July 1944 provided a unique opportunity for a small MO team in Italy to conduct one of the most successful operations of the war. "Sauerkraut" put a small team of trusted German POWs across the front lines in Italy to distribute MO leaflets about the assassination attempt in Wehrmacht rear areas. Private Barbara Lauwers interviewed potential agents from a nearby POW camp and 14 reliable men were recruited; a few days later – supplied with German uniforms, rifles, false identities and cover stories – these agents infiltrated enemy lines near Siena. Each carried 3,000 MO leaflets of a supposed proclamation by the German commander in Italy, Field Marshal Albert Kesselring, that he had resigned and that the war was lost. Each agent returned safely (with useful information about military positions) after posting the leaflets on walls, trees, trucks and in other places where they would draw attention from German soldiers.

This success prompted MO to send a dozen more "Sauerkraut" missions across the lines in Italy before the war ended. On one of these, agents distributed material from the "League of Lonely German Women," a fictitious organization conceived by Lauwers to weaken the resolve of German soldiers at the front. The members of the League were supposedly German women on the home front who would freely copulate with any German soldier on leave who showed her a pin made with the leaflet's heart-shaped logo; the purpose of this offer was supposedly to increase the birthrate for the Fatherland. More conventionally, MO in Italy also distributed leaflets and safe-conduct passes to persuade Czech conscripts and Italian soldiers to desert their units, and it was estimated that they successfully instigated the desertion of at least 10,000 enemy soldiers.

Other printed materials that MO employed were fake newspapers from imaginary German underground political parties opposed to the regime. *Das Neue Deutschland*, a newspaper from a fictitious peace party, was circulated among German troops in Italy, and *Der Oesterreicher* was purportedly produced by an Austrian resistance group. An MO team in Stockholm produced *Handel und Wandel*, a newsletter for businessmen who traveled between Sweden and Germany; printed from July 1944 to April 1945, it combined reliable business news with propaganda about the inevitable defeat of Germany. MO also successfully used the Germans' own propaganda leaflets against them. "Skorpion West" was a Wehrmacht operation in the fall of 1944 to drop leaflets promising final victory to encourage its soldiers to fight on; MO duplicated these leaflets with plenty of black propaganda designed to subvert this message, thus forcing the Germans to terminate this program.

In the Far East, MO was able to mail black messages directly to Japan in the summer of 1944 when a team based in New Delhi, India, came across a pouch of 475 postcards home, already passed by the Japanese Army censors, from soldiers of a Japanese unit that had since been wiped out. With the assistance of Nissei interpreters MO gently erased the original last messages home and replaced them with news of starvation and a sense of abandonment in the jungle. The altered cards were then placed in a pouch and left south of Mogaung in Burma for the Japanese to find and mail back home. The same MO unit was able to persuade Japanese soldiers in Burma to surrender by the use of forged Japanese Army documents; Elizabeth MacDonald came up with the idea of forging an order from the Japanese high command allowing troops in hopeless battle situations to surrender instead of fighting to the death. A perfect forgery was produced with the help of a Japanese POW; copies were slipped into Japanese-occupied Burma by Detachment 101, and air-dropped by the OWI. In China, MO was able to establish secret bases behind enemy lines to produce leaflets printed on local presses, which were distributed by Chinese agents and air-dropped by the US Army Fourteenth Air Force.

X-2 COUNTERESPIONAGE

Before X-2 was created in June 1943, SI handled all counterespionage matters. In response to a request by the OSS for access to Ultra decrypts, the British agreed on the condition that the OSS established its own self-contained counterespionage branch, which would be given exclusive access to Ultra and their counterespionage files. X-2 used its special status to check the backgrounds of potential OSS agents, reject proposed OSS operations on security grounds, protect OSS activities overseas from enemy penetration, operate directly against enemy operatives in neutral nations, and capture and turn enemy "stay-behind" agents in France and Italy. The operational headquarters of X-2 was established in London, due to its close proximity to Bletchley Park and the other Allied counterespionage services. While X-2 in London directed operations in Europe and the Mediterranean, X-2 in Washington directed counterespionage operations in the Far East.

R&A branch amassed a large library of German language materials as references for the reports that it produced for the OSS. Here a civilian employee at OSS headquarters in London browses a shelf of German books on law, administration and politics. (NARA)

One important source of intelligence was German newspapers obtained in neutral countries and sent to R&A branch for analysis. When the war made foreign publications harder to obtain, R&A initiated a joint effort with other government agencies to form the Interdepartmental Committee for the Acquisition of Foreign Publications, which maintained a steady supply of newspapers, serials, books and telephone directories collected by personnel in Allied and neutral capitals. German newspapers were gathered from Switzerland, Sweden and Turkey; Japanese publications from Argentina and China. One key benefit of R&A obtaining foreign publications was its ability to produce accurate statistics on German battle casualties, since German families were required to publish in their local newspapers the death notices of relatives killed in action. Even after the Germans stopped supplying newsagents abroad, individual subscribers in neutral countries still received their copies. (NARA)

X-2 in London was divided into geographic sections for Western Europe, the Iberian Peninsula, Scandinavia and the Middle East, each subdivided into desks dealing with specific countries. In March 1945 these desks shifted their focus to branches of the German Abwehr and Sicherheitsdienst intelligence services. Each of these desks collected and collated all available information into a central card registry that kept track of all persons of interest, and by 1945 the registry had over 400,000 entries. They were color-coded by category: pink for Abwehr or Sicherheitsdienst personnel, buff for political traitors and suspected collaborators, white for friendly persons, and blue for those still unclassified. X-2 focused on the operational procedures and working relationships of the German intelligence services, and on uncovering their plans for intelligence-gathering and sabotage; they were thus able to disrupt these operations directly through the employment of their SCI teams (see below). In late 1944, X-2 created the Art Looting Investigating Unit to help in the retrieval of items of value plundered by the Nazis, but its primary purpose was to obtain information on people who might use these ill-gotten treasures to fund Nazi activities after the war.

In the Far East, X-2 was only able to establish itself at Kunming, China in September 1944. It soon discovered that the Nationalist Chinese counterespionage effort against the Japanese by Gen Tai Li's BIS was unreliable or nonexistent. To overcome the obstacles of the BIS having sole authority to arrest enemy agents and the obvious limitations of American personnel operating in the field, X-2 recruited local Chinese agents; several networks were established in both occupied and unoccupied China, and successfully uncovered several Japanese spy rings. X-2 then turned this information over to the BIS, who neutralized these threats. The X-2 card file eventually contained 15,000 entries on people, organizations and places of interest. Despite this success, OSS bases and operations were effectively infiltrated by Communist Chinese agents.

Special Counter-Intelligence Units

To take rapid advantage of any intelligence-related opportunities during the Allied advance across France, X-2 established SCI teams that were attached to the G-2 of each US army and army group, working in cooperation with CIC personnel. Traveling just behind (or sometimes just ahead of) US units, their mission was to apply counterespionage information to protect Allied assets, neutralize enemy stay-behind agents, garner intelligence from captured enemy agents and documents, and debrief SI agents whom the advance caught up with. One SCI team captured the Gestapo HQ in Rennes complete with its personnel and files; another captured an Abwehr NCO who led them to several hidden caches of sabotage equipment for use against Allied installations.

As the Germans retreated from France they left stay-behind agents equipped with hidden radios to report on Allied movements; SCI units had to race to find these agents, not only to thwart this activity but also to obtain any valuable intelligence they might provide before they were caught and summarily executed by the resistance. X-2 in London provided the intercepts from enemy agents to the nearest SCI teams, who could then apprehend them and convince them that it was in their best interests to cooperate with X-2. A case officer was then assigned to control the turned agent, providing false information to be reported back to Berlin. This ruse was so effective that the Iron Cross was awarded *in absentia* to three turned agents.

RESEARCH & ANALYSIS

Donovan believed that academia could play an important intelligence role by using data and analysis to pinpoint enemy weak points. The R&A branch was thus and created divided into primary geographic divisions for Europe-Africa, Far East, USSR, and Latin America, each subdivided into economic, political, and specific geographic sections. R&A employed prominent historians, economists, sociologists, diplomats and other experts for their intellectual, analytical and research abilities. Materials from the Library of Congress, university libraries, research institutions, government agencies and from OSS agents in the field were used by R&A to produce reports either on demand or on its own initiative. These reports were provided to other OSS branches, the military and government agencies; they dealt with the military and economic potential of enemy and Allied countries, diplomatic issues, and supplementary information for the planning of military operations. In the summer of 1942 R&A was informed of Allied plans to invade North Africa; the entire staff worked day and night for several weeks to produce several detailed reports on Morocco, Algeria, and Tunisia, much to the astonished satisfaction of the military. R&A also produced the *Soldier's Guides* for American troops stationed overseas.

R&A established a Map Division that produced unique maps incorporating the economic, political and military situation of a specific country or area; information on these specially prepared maps included transportation routes, communications, industry, natural resources, terrain and weather. MD also amassed a large collection of foreign maps to assist with OSS operations overseas. The Central Information Division was created to collate R&A reports and other information for effective access; CID created a vast card catalog system that allowed it to provide extensive information at short notice. By 1945 over 3 million 3x5 cards, 300,000 captioned photographs, 300,000 classified intelligence documents, one

million maps, 350,000 foreign serial publications, 50,000 books, thousands of biographical files and 3,000 research studies had been compiled.

R&A also sent personnel overseas to directly distribute needed information, forward the latest intelligence to R&A headquarters in Washington, and help analyze data obtained in theater. Operating behind the Allied advance, R&A sought out important publications and reported on the economic and political issues in liberated areas. (Valuable industrial, technical, and military information regarding Japan was also uncovered in France and Italy.) R&A also traveled to former battlefields to examine German vehicles and equipment, recording factory markings and serial numbers; analysis of this information allowed R&A economists to estimate with a certain degree of accuracy the current production levels of equipment throughout occupied Europe. (The new location of an aircraft factory was found when R&A noticed that the inscription on a compass from a plane wreck had changed from "Focke-Wulf Bremen" to "Focke-Wulf Marienburg.") Such intelligence was passed on to the Enemy Objectives Unit based at the American Embassy in London, whose primary purpose was to identify critical targets for the strategic bombing campaign. Other intelligence used by EOU came from air reconnaissance, POW interrogations and agents operating on the Continent.

RESEARCH & DEVELOPMENT

Originally the Technical Development Section of SO, R&D became a separate branch in October 1942, to facilitate the development and production of special weapons and equipment used by OSS agents. Very few of these items were produced by R&D directly; it arranged for their development through contracts to government, academic and corporate laboratories. R&D established a working relationship with the National Defense Research Committee (which later became an advisory board to its successor, the Office of Scientific Research and Development), whose Division 19 enlisted the assistance of such laboratories. R&D's Technical Division observed the development of items to ensure they stayed within the bounds of reality, and then tested them to determine if they warranted full production. R&D also

B **REPORTING FROM THE FIELD**
1: "LINE-CROSSER"; SOUTHEAST FRANCE, SUMMER 1944
Local civilians and resistance fighters recruited by the OSS provided tactical intelligence such as the location of German positions, units and supply dumps. For short-range penetration operations these line-crossers would pass through the front lines on foot and return at a predetermined date and time to convey what they had seen. Others were provided with this standard military SCR-300 backpack radio (the original "walkie-talkie," although the term is now universally used for hand-held radios). It had a range of between three and five miles.

2: LIAISON WITH THE PARTISANS; CENTRAL YUGOSLAVIA, FALL 1943
Intelligence from deep within enemy territory was obtained by OSS liaisons with resistance groups such as Tito's Partisans (though the quality of the intelligence was at the mercy of the Partisans who provided it, and who saw it as a form of leverage.) This agent has started to prepare a coded message for his SSTR-1 suitcase radio. Although this was a successful design the power supply was a constant challenge; operators found that it used less battery power when transmitting than receiving messages. Inserted with a uniformed paramilitary group rather than operating undercover, this operator has no need to wear civilian clothing.

3: SI AGENT; GERMANY, SPRING 1945
One advantage enjoyed by OSS agents in Germany during the chaotic final months of the war was the Joan-Eleanor system; Joan was a hand-held transceiver that could communicate with an Eleanor-equipped Mosquito aircraft orbiting up to 30 miles away. This agent had to hold Joan no more than 3in from his mouth, and in the same exact spot to maintain the frequency and direction of the signal. Joan was best used in clear, flat fields or on high rooftops, as nearby metal and concrete structures degraded its performance.

obtained special devices from the British that were manufactured and supplied to the OSS. The Documentation Division of R&D was responsible for counterfeiting enemy documents for use by OSS agents in occupied territory. The Camouflage Division ensured that agents and their equipment remained inconspicuous; this included supplying European-style suitcases to carry clandestine radios, clothing suitable to the operational area, and the correct accessories to be carried in pockets.

FIELD PHOTOGRAPHIC

The Field Photographic branch was the brainchild of Hollywood director John Ford, who believed that a specialized unit of skilled cameramen would be a valuable asset in the support of military operations. Unofficially organized as a US Naval Reserve unit in 1939 (Ford had been a USNR officer since 1934), it was funded and equipped by Ford himself to document military activities and conduct photographic reconnaissance. Rebuffed by the US Navy, Field Photo did not become operational until it was recruited by Donovan for the COI in September 1941. Field Photo was part of SI when the OSS was established in June 1942, and did not become a separate branch until January 1943. Despite its predominantly naval character, personnel from all the military services were recruited into its ranks.

Field Photo made three types of films: special projects, strategic and documentary. The first were films specifically requested by the military or government agencies. Strategic photography involved filming and photographing geographical areas that had intelligence value. For instance, the Intelligence Photographic Documentation Project, a joint effort with R&A in 1944, created by means of air photography a large file of high-value military and industrial installations and important geographical areas in Europe and the Far East. The documentaries were training films for OSS

Academy Award-winning movie director John Ford led the Field Photographic Unit as a US Naval Reserve captain during the war, although personnel from all branches of the service were recruited; he is seen here near Milton Hall, England, in spring 1944. As well as many kinds of intelligence and instructional productions Field Photo documented actual OSS activities and other military operations around the world, from MO projects in Italy to Detachment 101 activities in Burma, and from the Doolittle Raid and the Japanese attack on Midway Island (where Ford was wounded) to the invasions of North Africa and Normandy. In total, Field Photo produced 87 films from 1940 to 1945. (NARA)

recruits that demonstrated weapons, equipment and techniques, or general instructional films on subjects as varied as the identification of enemy uniforms and life on the Japanese home islands. Field Photo also documented OSS and some other military operations worldwide.

COMMUNICATIONS
The small Code & Cable Section left over from COI had insufficient staff and resources to support clandestine operations overseas, and in September 1942 the Communications branch was established to provide training and communication channels for OSS operations. Military personnel and civilian amateur radio operators with the necessary skills were actively recruited. The Communications branch established a Research & Development Division (not to be confused with the separate R&D Branch) to devise special equipment for agents in the field, and developed and maintained the security of the codes and ciphers used by the OSS. The branch managed the radio traffic between field agents, overseas bases and OSS headquarters in Washington, which by 1944 was receiving 60,000 messages a month.

SPECIAL FUNDS
After its establishment by COI, Special Funds operated under various branches before becoming independent in May 1944. Its role was to finance secret OSS operations with funds that were not officially accounted for, in order to maintain security. Special Funds obtained intelligence on exchange rates, which currencies could or could not be used in particular places, foreign restrictions on the transfer of currency, and the financial situation of areas where agents operated (errors over the type and amount of currency they were provided could jeopardize a mission). Special Funds also paid sub-agents to conduct missions and covered their equipment costs and operational expenses, handled the salaries of civilian employees working in neutral countries, and provided currency to French and Italian resistance groups to finance their operations.

Special Funds obtained foreign currency through banks, brokers, and black market operations in neutral countries and North Africa. It also had to ensure that the money used in clandestine operations was not traceable. The Gestapo would record serial numbers or leave special markings on French francs before sending them into the black market to trap undercover agents; to avoid this, Special Funds examined all foreign currency against a list of all known marked notes. Fresh banknotes brought immediate suspicion upon an agent, so they were dumped on the floor and walked on until they became dirty and worn enough to be convincing. Gold was also obtained to purchase foreign currency, or as another medium of payment or bribery by agents, and in the Far East silver rupees and opium were also supplied. One of the greatest challenges Special Funds faced was from other OSS branches who believed that it had stockpiles of foreign money ready at a moment's notice; not realizing that considerable time and planning were involved, many OSS officers made requests to Special Funds only hours before their agents were to be dropped behind enemy lines.

MEDICAL SERVICES
Established as an independent branch in January 1944, Medical Services initially focused on ensuring proper medical care for OSS personnel at training areas and overseas bases. It also assessed the health situation of resistance

groups and provided them with medical supplies. Through these channels it was able to obtain intelligence about medical conditions in occupied territory, to forewarn Allied forces and relief agencies of any potential epidemics or other health-related concerns in areas soon to be liberated. Medical Services personnel also provided medical supplies to line-crossers as barter for information, and one side-benefit of its efforts was the ability to obtain political and other non-medical intelligence unavailable to other OSS branches. Medical Services examined abandoned German medical facilities and equipment to determine the health status of the Wehrmacht, and also gathered information on the Germans' potential to conduct chemical and biological warfare.

OPERATIONS

Given the passages above on Secret Intelligence, Special Operations and Operational Groups, in this chapter repetitive explanations of the exact functions of OSS missions are avoided. The information the OSS gathered behind the lines included the identification and location of enemy units, targets for Allied air power, and the local political and economic situation. Operations against the enemy in conjunction with resistance, partisan, and guerrilla groups were either indirect – through the sabotage of roads, railroad tracks, bridges, and communication lines – or direct, through the ambush of convoys and the harassment of enemy units and outposts. The OSS also organized, trained, supplied, and advised these irregular formations to directly support Allied operations by attacking enemy positions, capturing towns, rescuing downed Allied airmen, and seizing bridges, power stations, and dams before they could be destroyed by the retreating enemy.

North Africa

In the spring of 1941 the still-neutral United States concluded an agreement allowing the Vichy French to purchase food, oil and other necessities for their colonies in North Africa. To ensure these materials did not end up in Axis hands a dozen vice-consuls were stationed that summer in Casablanca, Oran, Algiers and Tunis to serve as control officers. Although officially working for the State Department, these men were chosen for their intelligence-gathering skills; but it was not until January 1942, when Donovan sent USMC Col William A. Eddy to Tangier as the new naval attaché, that the intelligence efforts of the vice-consuls were coordinated. Eddy had all the intelligence sent to him via diplomatic pouch and a network of hidden radios operated by the vice-consuls, forwarding the information to Washington. During the planning stages of Operation "Torch" the vice-consuls and other OSS agents reported the status of Vichy French forces, ports, airfields and terrain. Two OSS agents smuggled the pro-Allied René Malvergne, chief pilot of Port Lyautey, from Casablanca to Tangier, and during "Torch" Malvergne piloted the destroyer USS *Dallas* under fire up the Sebou river and landed a US Ranger detachment who seized the airfield near Port Lyautey. Contacts were established to organize resistance groups to seize key installations and perform sabotage in support of the invasion. When "Torch" commenced on November 8, 1942 the resistance sabotaged communication lines and occupied several important buildings, but Vichy French troops were able to recapture them before American soldiers could arrive. When US forces landed along the North African coasts they came prepared by the intelligence gathered by the OSS, and were met on the beach by its agents to help guide them inland.

While the Allies fought the Afrika Korps across Tunisia in the spring of 1943, a small SO detachment carried out sabotage and raids, and reconnaissance either in person or through the coercion of local Arabs. During the German offensive towards Kasserine Pass the detachment's abilities were squandered in performing infantry combat roles, and attrition from wounds and several captures forced their withdrawal in late March 1943.

NEUTRAL COUNTRIES
Switzerland

Surrounded on all sides by enemy territory, Switzerland became one of the best sources of intelligence for the OSS. In November 1942 a small SI mission was set up at the American Legation in Bern headed by Allen Dulles, who arrived via Vichy France just as the Germans were occupying the rest of that country in response to Operation "Torch." With contacts established from his pre-war years in a Wall Street law office, and by discreet meetings with visitors to his apartment at Herrengasse 23, Dulles established a reliable network of sources. Intelligence was obtained on Germany's military and industrial capabilities, secret weapons research, the persecution of Jews and prior warning of the July 1944 plot against Hitler's life. One of the biggest intelligence coups of the war was achieved when Fritz Kolbe, an assistant to the Foreign Office liaison to the German High Command, voluntarily provided Dulles with copies of secret diplomatic cables sent to Berlin from its overseas posts. The amount of material that Kolbe would provide (1,600 cables by war's end) strained the limited resources of the small OSS mission to translate and report their contents to Washington. Other information to

The Air Crew Rescue Unit was formed in summer 1944 to evacuate Allied airmen forced down in either Partisan or Chetnik territory in Yugoslavia. Lt Nick Lalich (left), team leader of the "Halyard" Mission with Lt Mike Rajacich (right), is interviewing a P-51 pilot who was shot down south of Belgrade in September 1944. Their names are a reminder that the OSS sought out Americans of suitable national heritage to operate in particular countries. Rajacich wears British parachute wings on his left chest, while Lalich has a British holster. (NARA)

OSS headquarters was sent via the radio at the American Embassy, and nightly via a radiotelephone that Dulles had to use cautiously in the knowledge that it was tapped by Swiss intelligence. Sending actual documents was impossible until the summer of 1944 when Allied forces reached the Swiss border.

In late February 1945, SS Gen Karl Wolff, the commander of SS and Police units in Italy, conveyed to Dulles a desire to surrender all German forces in his jurisdiction. Political complications between the Western Allies and the Soviet Union, and Wolff's attempts to obtain the parallel capitulation of German Army Group C, caused delays, but Dulles remained an important conduit in this process until May 2, 1945, when all German and Fascist forces in Italy surrendered unconditionally, six days before V-E Day.

Spain

During World War II Gen Franco's Spanish regime naturally maintained close ties with the Reich. The first SI agents inserted in April 1942 were tasked with discovering what economic and military aid Spain provided to Germany, and if the Germans might cross into Spanish territory either with or without Franco's agreement. After the Allies pressured Spain to stop sending raw materials to Germany the OSS uncovered smuggling rings that were soon shut down by the Spanish. From January 1943, SI personnel stationed in Barcelona and Bilbao established networks in southern France with agents recruited from the French resistance and Spanish Republican exiles. The use of couriers across the Pyrenees mountains allowed the physical removal from France of bulky items and documents with information that could not easily be transmitted by radio. SI in Spain provided about half of the reports on the German defenses and units in southern France in preparation for the Allied landings there in August 1944.

Sweden

After its first agent arrived in Stockholm in March 1942 the OSS used this central location to support its operations in Scandinavia and into Germany itself. Local sub-agents were recruited to infiltrate into Denmark and Norway, and outposts set up in the ports of Malmö, Helsingborg and Göteborg interviewed travelers for any useful intelligence and observed German shipping to and from Norway. One important result of the latter missions was the discovery that Sweden was shipping a larger quantity of ball bearings to Germany than it had revealed, and OSS reports allowed the Allies to obtain an agreement from the Swedes to cease all ball-bearing shipments. The OSS recruited a Swedish oil dealer who in October 1944 toured several of Germany's synthetic oil plants on the pretext that he was establishing one in Sweden that would benefit the Reich's war effort; his reports instead proved helpful to the Allied strategic bombing effort.

In August 1944, SO began to set up the first of six supply bases just inside Swedish territory along the Norwegian border. Code-named "Sepals," these provided supplies and a communications link with London for the Norwegian resistance, with the tacit approval of the Swedish government. Weapons and equipment were flown into Stockholm in unarmed B-24 Liberators of the Air Transport Command, and driven to the Sepals with the cooperation of the Swedish Army and police.

Hennings Jessen-Schmidt, a member of the Danish resistance working for SO, infiltrated Berlin by way of Denmark and Hamburg in March 1945. He established a safe house and bought an automobile in preparation for

SO operated six Sepal supply bases along the Norwegian border in Sweden in the final months of the war with the tacit approval of the Swedish government. Here operatives from a Sepal clown for the camera behind two Swedish border guards and a prisoner from an Organization Todt unit at Narvik. (NARA)

sabotage operations around the capital when the rest of his SO team could join him. Unfortunately, they were still stuck in Denmark when the British liberated it. Jessen-Schmidt was able to send four reports back to Stockholm via courier about the chaotic situation around Berlin until the Red Army occupied the city in May 1945.

ITALY & THE WESTERN MEDITERRANEAN
Corsica, Sardinia & Sicily
The next OSS operation after Operation "Torch" came in December 1942 when an SI team landed in southern Corsica from the French submarine *Casabianca*, subsequently radioing reports on enemy occupation forces until their capture in May 1943. After the Italian Armistice in September 1943 the French resistance or "Maquis" on Corsica rose up, and a hastily assembled Free French force along with a small SI/OG team assisted in the island's liberation. SI organized the Maquis in gathering current intelligence, while the OG team assisted French troops in harassing the withdrawing Germans until they completely abandoned Corsica in October 1943.

In June 1943 an SI team were landed in northwestern Sardinia by PT boat, but they were quickly captured by the Italians. After the Italian Armistice a small SO/OG team parachuted into southern Sardinia and made arrangements with the Italians for the arrival of American occupation forces.

The OSS was forbidden from infiltrating teams into Sicily before the Allied invasion in July 1943 so as to avoid alerting the Germans. The small OSS team that followed the troops ashore were inexperienced in gathering tactical information, and locally recruited line-crossers accomplished very little; one ill-conceived operation behind Axis lines resulted in the capture of the head of the SO unit.

Italy
When the US Fifth Army landed at Salerno in September 1943 the OSS units attached to it were better prepared to provide tactical intelligence; refugees

The inter-Allied Jedburgh teams in France used a mixture of US and British equipment. While the American "Jed" in left foreground wears the M42 US paratrooper jump uniform the others are wearing British battledress and 1937-pattern webbing – see Plate C2. Note the Special Force wings on the American's right shoulder; he also has a scabbarded Sykes-Fairbairn knife on his pistol belt behind his holster. Team "Ronald," seen here, operated in Brittany in August–September 1944. (NARA)

were interrogated and recruited as line-crossers to report on the location of German units. Throughout the Italian campaign the OSS recruited agents for short-range penetration missions, and to establish networks for the coordination of intelligence-gathering and sabotage with partisan groups. These Italian agents included partisans, military personnel, and people working for the pro-Allied faction of the Servizio Informazioni Militare intelligence service. These agents infiltrated occupied Italy either on foot, by torpedo boat or parachute. The OSS established a network in Rome made up

C SPECIAL OPERATIONS

1: "CAMEL" TEAM; SOUTHEAST CHINA, SPRING 1945

Many SO personnel in China wore Nationalist Chinese uniforms, like this heavy cotton padded jacket and trousers, to better blend in with the guerrilla units they directed. Despite their success in ambushing Japanese convoys and demolishing bridges, SO found many inexperienced guerrillas reluctant to engage the Japanese or lacking in fire discipline. The "Camel" Team overcame this with both training and a prize system that awarded extra ammunition or grenades for killing a certain number of Japanese. Submachine guns were awarded for any Japanese soldiers captured alive. **(Inset)** Chinese Nationalist cap badge.

2: JEDBURGH; CENTRAL FRANCE, SUMMER 1944

The inter-Allied Jedburgh teams wore a mixture of Allied uniforms while operating in France. While American members normally wore US uniforms, some, like this OSS man, did wear British battledress; note the SF jump wings on his right sleeve and the 48-star US flag patch on his left. He is loading .303in rounds into a magazine for the Bren LMG at his feet before he instructs members of a Maquis group how to operate it. The Jedburghs trained, supplied and organized French resistance groups, and joined them in direct action against the Germans.

3: "UNION II" MISSION; SOUTHERN FRANCE, SUMMER 1944

"Union II" was an SO mission predominantly composed of US Marine Corps personnel. Each member parachuted from a separate B-17 during a supply mission to the French Maquis group that they were sent to train. "Union II" continued after several of its members, including its leader Maj Peter Ortiz, were captured by the Germans. Only the forest-green garrison cap identifies this operative's service; **(inset)** USMC cap badge. He wears a Parsons ("M41") field jacket, OD wool shirt and pants, and M42 Corcoran jump boots; note the SF jump wings worn here on the left chest. He carries an M1A1 carbine.

1

2

3

of Italian resistance leaders and military officers, which began transmitting reports in November 1943. OSS agent Peter Tompkins arrived in Rome in late January 1944 to coordinate operations in anticipation of the city's liberation by Allied forces landing at Anzio, and after the Germans contained the beachhead Tompkins radioed reports of troop movements through the capital that helped warn the Allies of forthcoming assaults.

From October 1943, OG teams based on Corsica established observation posts on several islands off Italy's Tyrrhenian coast to report on German shipping. OG raiding and reconnaissance parties operated against other islands and along the Italian coast until March 1944, when the "Ginny II" Mission were captured and executed by the Germans. From June 1944 to the end of the war MU officers commanded a volunteer contingent of Italian "San Marco" Marines that infiltrated and recovered agents, supplied partisan groups, and conducted sabotage along Italy's Adriatic coast. In August 1944, while the Allies advanced up the Italian peninsula, OG teams parachuted into the northern half of the country to train, supply, and coordinate the activities of the partisans, to include attacking German troops in direct support of the US Fifth Army. Although winter saw the Allies pause in front of the Gothic Line, OG teams continued operations and skirmished with German anti-partisan sweeps. When the final Allied offensive began in April 1945, OG teams blocked and ambushed retreating enemy columns and, alongside the partisans, seized important sites and facilities before they could be destroyed. Partisans cleared entire areas of Germans, cut several highways to block their retreat, and liberated several cities before the arrival of Allied troops.

THE BALKANS
Yugoslavia
The OSS found itself in the middle of a quasi-civil war in Yugoslavia between Josip Tito's Communist Partisans and Gen Draza Mihailovich's royalist Chetniks. In order to assess all local efforts against the Axis occupation and to obtain intelligence in-country, in August 1943 OSS liaison officers were parachuted in to both these guerrilla movements to report on their activities and capabilities. In October 1943 MU gathered a small fleet of schooners and other cargo vessels at the Italian ports of Bari and Monopoli, and shipped supplies to the Partisan-held island of Vis off the Yugoslavian coast until January 1944. Some of the Allied arms supplied to Tito were not used against the Germans, as several OSS personnel with the Chetniks discovered. From January to August 1944 OG teams and British Commandos conducted several reconnaissance and raiding operations in the Dalmatian Islands to harass the German garrisons. The first penetration of the Third Reich by the OSS occurred in June 1944, when Maj Franklin Lindsay and a band of Partisans crossed into an annexed portion of northern Slovenia, successfully blowing a 150ft gap in a stone viaduct bridge and cutting an important rail line for the rest of the war.

At the Tehran Conference in November 1943 the decision was taken to cease all aid to Mihailovich and instead to fully support Tito; the reason was the Chetniks' less than aggressive guerrilla campaign, and charges of collaboration with the enemy. Mihailovich claimed that a lack of supplies and fear of wholesale reprisals against civilians prevented him from fighting the Germans at the level the Allies demanded, but the decision stuck, and the OSS was forced to withdraw its last liaison officer with the Chetniks in May 1944. That summer, however, a large number of American airmen continued to bail out over Chetnik-held areas. In collaboration with the USAAF, the OSS established the ACRU that parachuted into Chetnik territory in August 1944; the unit built a rough airstrip that enabled C-47s to evacuate over 500 Allied airmen by the time it departed in December.

When the Red Army crossed into Yugoslavia in September 1944, and as more territory came under Partisan control, Tito imposed severe restrictions on the movement and activities of the OSS teams that prevented them from gathering any useful intelligence for the rest of the war. The OSS established a mission in Belgrade after it was liberated in October 1944, and reported on political, economic, and medical conditions there before withdrawing in July 1945.

Albania

The first SI team landed on the coast of this small and undeveloped nation in November 1943, and established a small headquarters in a nearby cave called "Seaview." Other SI teams served as liaisons with Enver Hoxha's Communist partisans fighting the Germans until the capital, Tirana, was liberated in November 1944. The only SO mission occurred when Capt Lloyd G. Smith arrived in December 1943 to search for 30 passengers of a USAAF C-53 transport that had crash-landed the previous month. Albanian civilians and SOE officers guided the survivors (who included ten of 13 US Army flight nurses) to southern Albania, where Smith met them and led them to "Seaview" for evacuation to Italy in January 1944. Smith arranged for the remaining three nurses to be driven from their hideout to the coast and safety the following March.

It takes a special kind of bravery to operate in enemy-occupied territory, and especially while wearing full USMC uniform. Capt Peter Ortiz is seen here consulting with the local Maquis as part of the inter-Allied "Union" Mission in early 1944. (NARA)

Greece

SI teams operated throughout Greece from August 1943, either independently or in liaison with the nationalist EDES or Communist EAM/ELAS guerrillas. SO personnel led Greek guerrillas in sabotage and ambushes; one of the most successful SO operations of the war occurred when the "Chicago" Mission cut off the export of chrome ore from Turkey to Germany by blowing up the Alexandroupolis and Svilengrad bridges simultaneously on the night of May 27, 1944. MU sustained OSS operations by transporting personnel and supplies in fishing boats (caiques) from a secret base that Turkey allowed them to establish at Rema Bay on its western coast. From April 1944, OG teams were deployed to work with guerrillas in hampering the Germans from withdrawing units that might reinforce Normandy against the forthcoming invasion. OG operations continued until the Germans withdrew from Greece by the end of October 1944.

FRANCE & THE LOW COUNTRIES
Secret Intelligence

February 1943 saw the first OSS agent (independent of any particular branch) infiltrate France from the French submarine *Casabianca* to set up a clandestine radio station in the southern port of Toulon. Other radio stations followed, and while they eventually fell under the jurisdiction of SI, the first official penetration into France by that branch came in August 1943 when the "Penny-Farthing" team parachuted in and set up a base in Lyon. As more SI teams landed in southern France, chains of sub-agents were formed, their information being either radioed to OSS headquarters in Algiers or sent by courier across the Pyrenees to OSS stations in Spain. Intelligence gathered by these networks played a key role in the successful Allied landings on the Riviera coast in August 1944.

Maj Peter Ortiz (second from left) returned to France as head of the "Union II" Mission that landed in the French Alps on August 1, 1944. Weeks later, Ortiz and three teammates were surrounded while fighting in the village of Centron; they surrendered after the Germans agreed to spare the village. (NARA)

Armed here with a Marlin SMG, 2nd Lt Herbert Brucker (second from left) served as the radio operator in the SO "Hermit" Circuit in central France from May to September 1944. "Hermit" helped arm and train local resistance groups to conduct sabotage, eliminate collaborators, and openly engage German forces when liberation drew close. (Walter O'Brien Collection, ARSOF Archives, JFK Special Warfare Museum)

In the more challenging environment of occupied northern France, SI participated in a joint operation with the British SIS called "Sussex," whereby two-man teams of an observer and a radio operator were placed near rail yards, road intersections, airfields and river crossings to report on German movements. The first Sussex teams were parachuted in April 1944 and, by the use of sub-agents, began reporting on the location of German units, supply dumps and V-1 launching sites; some of these targets were bombed not long afterwards. After the Normandy landings SI initiated Operation "Proust," by which agents gathered tactical intelligence at the direct request of US armies. They would rendezvous with the French Maquis to locate the enemy, and the Proust agent would then report to the Special Force Detachment (see below) attached to the specific army for which the agent was gathering information.

As the US First Army advanced into Belgium, its SF Detachment recruited resistance fighters from the Belgian Secret Army to scout, gather intelligence and mop up bypassed German pockets. Despite this accomplishment the G-2 at US First Army did not hold the SF Detachment in high regard, and obtained its withdrawal in September 1944 – a decision that contributed to the First Army being caught off guard by the German offensive in the Ardennes the following December.

In September 1944 the SI "Melanie" Mission deployed to Eindhoven in Holland to report the intelligence gathered by the various Dutch resistance groups and by line-crossers.

Special Force Detachments

SF Detachments were established in January 1944 to coordinate the operations of each US army and army group with OSS teams and resistance forces operating in their areas. The detachments contained personnel from SI and SO who worked under the G-2 and G-3 of each army or army group respectively; they passed on pertinent intelligence received from either agents in the field or the resistance, or forwarded from London. In August 1944, as the US Army approached Paris, SI in London provided the latest locations of German military depots in the French capital 36 hours after the request was received

RAF personnel help members of OG "Patrick" prepare for a drop into central France in August 1944. Led by 53-year-old LtCol Serge Obolensky, "Patrick" was successful in securing the hydroelectric plant at Eguzon before the retreating Germans could destroy it. (NARA)

from an SF Detachment. Agents locally recruited by SF Detachments were sent behind the lines either on foot or by parachute to obtain information specifically requested by US Army units, and sabotage and ambushes by the resistance were also arranged to support offensive operations. SF Detachments also debriefed OSS agents and teams and resistance fighters after advancing American forces overran them.

Special Operations

The first SO agents to land in France in June 1943 were instructors and radio operators to provide assistance to British SOE "F-Circuits" already in place. Each F-Circuit normally had an organizer, his lieutenant and a radio operator, and recruited, trained and equipped resistance fighters in its region. SO personnel operated in many SOE F-Circuits, and also established several of their own beginning with "Sacristan" in June 1943. Virginia Hall, who had previously worked undercover in Vichy France for the SOE, organized the only SO circuit to be led by a woman. Hall armed over 400 Maquis who conducted ambushes, derailed several trains in their tunnels, and demolished several railroad bridges in the summer of 1944.

Operation "Jedburgh" was a joint effort between SO, SOE and the Free French to establish three-man teams that could quickly organize, supply, train and accompany resistance groups in direct support of advancing Allied armies. In contrast to the regionally rooted F-Circuits, Jedburghs could be parachuted anywhere in France depending on the battlefield situation. To avoid alerting the Germans, Gen Eisenhower forbade the first Jedburgh team from deploying to France until the night of the Normandy invasion, but soon afterwards teams began parachuting across France. (The Jedburghs were also successful in keeping resistance groups of different political loyalties focused on fighting the Germans instead of each other.)

In August 1944 additional Jedburgh teams were parachuted in to protect Gen Patton's flanks as his troops simultaneously advanced on the port city of Brest and towards the German border, organizing local resistance groups to block and harass German units. Many Jedburgh teams were unable to fulfill their mission because they were overrun by the faster-than-expected American advance.

In September 1944 Jedburgh teams were attached to the airborne divisions in Operation "Market Garden" in Holland, to recruit the local Dutch resistance to provide assistance and intelligence and to establish a communications link between the airborne forces and SFHQ in London. The Jedburghs landed along with the paratroopers, which did not allow them sufficient time; many of their radios were lost or damaged, and most teams were unable to fulfill their missions due to the incessant German attacks along the airborne perimeters, though Jedburghs near Nijmegen were more successful. The tri-national Jedburgh team "Dudley" was deployed separately in eastern Holland; it conducted intelligence and sabotage operations, but by the end of 1944 its effectiveness had suffered from disunity among Dutch resistance groups and from German countermeasures.

Operational Groups

From June to September 1944, OG teams openly engaged the Germans in infrastructure sabotage and ambushes; paradoxically, they also seized

Despite years of German occupation transportation was available to OSS teams such as OG "Alice" in southern France, thanks to local resistance groups and cooperative civilians. Note the M1A1 bazooka stowed upright behind the truck cab. (Francis Coleman Collection, ARSOF Archives, JFK Special Warfare Museum)

hydroelectric plants and dams to prevent their destruction. On some of these missions OG teams operated alongside the British SAS, inter-Allied Jedburgh teams and the French resistance, which they also supplied and trained. With help from the Maquis, OG teams were able to exaggerate their size and bluff entire German garrisons into surrendering; this tactic successfully convinced more than 10,000 Germans to surrender out of the belief that the Americans would treat them better than the French.

CZECHOSLOVAKIA

The Slovak National Uprising in late August 1944 saw dissident Slovak Army units and partisans rise against the pro-German regime to seize large areas of central and eastern Slovakia. Seeing an opportunity to penetrate central Europe, the OSS hastily assembled the "Dawes" Mission to fly into Tri Duby airfield in B-17s in mid September. Arriving with supplies for the Slovak fighters, the OSS team radioed intelligence reports and evacuated downed Allied airmen. A Waffen-SS counteroffensive crushed the uprising by late October and, unable to evacuate in time, the "Dawes" Mission fled eastwards across the Tatra Mountains in grim winter conditions, guided by their interpreter Maria Gulovich. Most of them, and the accompanying SOE "Windproof" Mission, were captured in a cabin by the Abwehr's 218 Antipartisan Unit on December 26. They were taken to Mauthausen concentration camp, interrogated under torture, and finally shot in January 1945. Gulovich, two OSS personnel and two others from the SOE team were in another cabin at the time of the capture; in February 1945 they reached Red Army lines and eventual safety.

NORWAY

Since the SOE had been working with Milorg, the Norwegian resistance movement, since the early days of the German occupation, the OSS played only a supporting role in the final months of the war. The SO "Westfield" Mission in Stockholm began establishing the Sepal supply bases along the Norwegian border north of the 62nd Parallel in August 1944 (see above). Located just inside Sweden, the Sepals were manned by Norwegians recruited by SO; they kept the Milorg supplied, radioed intelligence to London, and

---

D

OPERATIONAL GROUPS
1: FRANCE, SUMMER 1944

In contrast to other OSS branches the role of Operational Groups was to engage with the enemy directly; they thus wore conventional uniform, although they were unlikely to receive the treatment guaranteed by the Geneva Convention if they fell into German hands. This OG member wears an M1943 field jacket and OD wool trousers, and is armed with an M1 carbine and grenades in a triple tie-down pouch. The sight of OG teams miles behind enemy lines helped boost the morale of the French population, who knew liberation was not far off, and the teams' ability to speak the language of the country in which they operated was an important asset.

2: GREECE, SUMMER 1944

Greek OG teams were made up of volunteers from the US Army's 122nd (Greek) Infantry Battalion. Sent to Greece in the spring of 1944, their mission was to hinder the redeployment of German occupation forces from that country to the fighting fronts, and was accomplished through the destruction of bridges, railroad tracks and convoys. Greek OG teams discovered that an effective way to immobilize a locomotive was to place a bazooka round into its boiler; this Tech 5 is armed with an M1A1 bazooka, and is wearing a paratrooper's M42 "jump jacket" with OD wool trousers and Corcorans.

3: NORWAY, SPRING 1945

Composed of ethnic Norwegians who volunteered from the US Army's 99th (Norwegian) Infantry Battalion, a Norwegian OG team in fact first saw action in France in the summer of 1944. They were sent next to Norway in March 1945 to help prevent the Germans from withdrawing reinforcements for the fighting fronts by rail. This OG man on patrol is wearing a US Army ski parka with fur-trimmed hood, ski trousers and ski-mountain boots, and has an M1 Garand slung over his shoulder.

Organized and led by Maj Aaron Bank (center, wearing belt), German soldiers with anti-Nazi sympathies were recruited from POW camps and trained for Operation "Iron Cross," a plan to drop a 50-man SO unit in German uniforms to seize Hitler and other Nazi leaders who might flee into a National Redoubt in the Austrian Alps in spring 1945. Hitler never left Berlin, the Redoubt never existed, and "Iron Cross" was never activated. (Aaron Bank Collection, ARSOF Archives, JFK Special Warfare Museum)

skirmished with German patrols inside Norway. In October 1944 the Allies directed the Milorg to commence the sabotage of transportation links throughout the country to hinder the Germans from sending reinforcements to the fighting fronts, and this was deemed an appropriate mission for the Norwegian OG that had already seen action in France. In late March 1945 an OG team led by Maj William E. Colby parachuted into central Norway to sabotage the Nordland rail line; with the roads snowbound, this would force 150,000 German troops in northern Norway to take the slower route by sea. One "Carpetbagger" B-24 accidentally dropped its stick into Sweden, but they were later allowed to rejoin their team in Norway. Initially assigned to demolish the Grana Bridge, his limited number of personnel forced Colby to blow the less well-defended railway bridge at Tangen and destroy 2.5km of track in two separate operations in April 1945.

GERMANY

The OSS did not infiltrate SI agents into Germany itself until the last months of the war due to several factors. The OSS had already established several contacts within Germany via its outposts in neutral countries; most of its resources were focused on supporting the liberation of France; and Allied victories in summer 1944 convinced many that Germany would surrender before the OSS needed to penetrate it. The lack of a certifiable German resistance movement and the tight Gestapo security apparatus posed serious challenges to the insertion of agents; as the front lines solidified along the German frontier that autumn, attempts by the different SF Detachments to use line-crossers to obtain intelligence met with little success. The exception was the SF Detachment with the US Seventh Army in the Alsace region of France, which was unique in supplying civilian clothing and forged documents to its agents. German POWs with anti-Nazi leanings were recruited as line-crossers, and the first infiltrated and returned safely in December 1944. Mines and crossfire along the front lines took a toll, so the detachment initiated (with some success)

"Tourist" missions, whereby agents were parachuted at least 50 miles behind the front and gathered information on their way back to American lines.

The SI agents parachuted into the Reich included German socialists, Communists and former POWs; the first was Jupp Kappius, who landed in the Ruhr in September 1944. French, Dutch, Belgian and Polish agents were also enlisted with the cooperation of their respective intelligence services to pose as conscripted laborers. Very few Americans were parachuted into Germany. At the start of 1945 intelligence-gathering agents began dropping blind across Germany, and some teams even threatened German communities with air raids if they did not provide useful intelligence. Two French women forced into prostitution assisted two Belgian agents in Regensburg by allowing them to hide in a closet and write down information that the women coaxed out of their German clients. Two agents who parachuted outside Berlin in March 1945 recruited a small network of family and friends that reported several industrial and rail targets; when the Red Army entered the capital the following month the agents attempted to assist by capturing a bridge, but it was destroyed in the process.

Teams landed in Austria obtained useful intelligence and support from the burgeoning resistance movement. They included the "Greenup" team near Innsbruck, which reported on underground factories, rail traffic (thus helping the USAAF to block the Brenner Pass), and the reported but ultimately fictitious Nazi National Redoubt in the Alps. Corporal Frederick Mayer, who led Greenup, posed as a wounded German lieutenant in an officers' club and reported the location and details of the Führerbunker in Berlin. After being captured and tortured by the Gestapo, Mayer convinced Franz Hofer, the local Gauleiter, to surrender Innsbruck to the US Army without a fight in May 1945.

Special Force Detachments were established in early 1944 to coordinate OSS activities with the operations of each of the American armies in Northwest Europe. The success of Gen Patton's rapid advance across France in the summer of 1944 was due in part to the resistance activities coordinated by the OSS on his southern flank. Here a convoy from SF Detachment 11 is leaving Third Army's headquarters at Chalons sur Marne as the advance continues eastward. Nothing in their uniforms or equipment sets them apart as OSS personnel. (NARA)

OPPOSITE TOP It got chilly
in the mountainous areas of
Burma, particularly at night;
this member of Detachment
101 armed with a Marlin wears
a pullover sweater. (Courtesy
Ian Grimwood)

BELOW Many in Detachment
101 went shirtless in the humid
Burmese jungle so that they
could quickly remove any
leeches that fell upon them
from the thick vegetation.
(Walter O'Brien Collection,
ARSOF Archives, JFK Special
Warfare Museum)

Although most of the agents sent into Germany were unable to send their reports due to broken radio sets, they were finally able to provide their information when overrun by American troops. Their skills and abilities, the quality of their forged documents, and the chaos surrounding them during the last days of the Third Reich allowed all but a few agents to evade the Gestapo.

SOUTHEAST ASIA & THE PACIFIC
Burma

Detachment 101 was the first SO unit deployed overseas, and recruited indigenous tribesmen in Burma for espionage, sabotage and guerrilla warfare. This irregular campaign helped the Allies reopen the Burma Road to China and liberate the country from Japanese occupation. Detachment 101 established its base at a tea plantation near Nazira in eastern India in October 1942, and trained British, Burmese, Anglo-Burmese and Anglo-Indian agents in intelligence-gathering and sabotage. The Air Transport Command agreed to drop supplies and personnel behind the lines in return for Detachment 101 helping to rescue downed airmen. The first agents infiltrated Burma in January 1943 to report intelligence, carry out sabotage and guide Allied bombers to Japanese targets. Some of the bases established behind the lines had rough airstrips used by light planes to bring in visitors and evacuate the wounded. From these bases Detachment 101 recruited the Kachins of northern Burma, who were very familiar with the jungle terrain; once trained, they became effective guerrillas and radio operators. (Kachin loyalty stemmed from their pre-war relationship with Christian missionaries, from the medical care provided for them.) Nissei personnel in Detachment 101 interrogated Japanese captured in these operations, and also led Kachins into action, but only after their faces were carefully studied to avoid them being mistaken for the enemy.

In the spring of 1944, Detachment 101 supported Allied offensives into Burma with Kachin battalions scouting ahead of Allied units, providing flank protection and attacking Japanese lines of communication. The Arakan Field

BELOW Detachment 101 was able to recruit a large number of Kachin tribesmen, who welcomed the opportunity to fight their harsh Japanese occupiers (at times American personnel had to curtail their enthusiasm, forbidding them to collect the ears from Japanese corpses). Lt Ralph Yempku was a Nissei who led a company of Kachin Rangers in central Burma in late 1944, setting ambushes and interrogating Japanese prisoners. In the OSS, Nissei also fought with Chinese guerrillas and helped produce MO material. (Courtesy Ian Grimwood)

Unit – composed of SI, OG, and MU personnel from Detachment 404 – surveyed beaches and rivers along the Burmese coast, dropped off agents and supported several British landings in the spring of 1945. Based in Ceylon, the AFU was absorbed by Detachment 101 in March 1945. The following month Detachment 101, with close air support, began to single-handedly clear eastern Burma to make the Burma Road secure. It also harassed the Japanese retreat along the Taunggyi–Kentung road into Thailand, and the seizure of several key towns finally severed the road completely in June 1945. With the Japanese forced out of Burma, Detachment 101 was disbanded in July 1945.

Thailand

As one of the few independent countries in Asia, Thailand formed an alliance with Japan to maintain its autonomy, declaring war on the United States in January 1942. This declaration was not reciprocated, and the OSS recruited agents from the pro-Allied Free Thai movement. Chinese obstruction delayed plans to infiltrate Free Thai agents overland, and those who were finally inserted in June 1944 were either killed or captured by Thai police. Shortly afterwards the pro-Japanese government was replaced by one headed by

Supply by air was the only way to sustain Detachment 101 operations. Most supplies were dropped in locally made wicker baskets, but less fragile items like clothing and rice were "free-dropped" in sacks without parachutes. (These falling bags were dangerous, for they destroyed huts and killed people on impact.) Here a large supply of K-rations dropped to a Kachin Rangers unit is being gathered in the middle of the drop zone. The parachute canopies were kept as markers to signal cargo planes on future supply drops, or given to local villagers as rewards for their support. (Courtesy Ian Grimwood)

Pridi Phanomyong, a secret supporter of the Allies. In September 1944 a Free Thai agent was parachuted in to make OSS contact with Pridi, who had one of the captured agents radio his favorable reply. In January 1945 OSS officers Richard Greenlee and John Wester landed in the Gulf of Thailand from an RAF Catalina and reached Pridi's residence undetected, and Pridi agreed to pass on intelligence to be radioed back by SI agents in Bangkok to Detachment 404 in Ceylon. Unfortunately the information supplied was of little value before SI officers shared intelligence-gathering techniques. Free Thai agents also set up a network across Thailand to radio intelligence back to Ceylon. To

Late 1944: a squad of Kachin Rangers pause in a clearing south of Myitkyina. Some wear their American-supplied uniforms and jungle boots while others keep their native dress. Footwear represented prestige, so some Kachins stayed barefoot in the field and wore their boots only in their home villages. (US Army Military History Institute)

show support for the Thai underground and to maintain the flow of intelligence, secret bases staffed by SO and MU instructors were established throughout the country, supplied either by parachute or by C-47s landing at hidden airfields. Japan knew of these activities, but could not counter them effectively before the end of the war in August 1945.

French Indochina

OSS plans to penetrate French Indochina directly had little success. The independent Gordon-Bernard-Tan intelligence network provided the only

As Detachment 101 moved further south in 1945 units of Kachin Rangers operated in larger numbers in a more conventional role. Here a company of Kachins is seen south of Lashio while marching down a road heavily used by Japanese trucks. Detachment 101 saw its bloodiest fighting in southeastern Burma as it fought to clear the area of Japanese troops and cut their evacuation route into Thailand. By that time Chinese, Burmese, Karens, Shans, Nagas and other peoples were being recruited into its ranks. (Joseph M. Straub Collection, US Army Military History Institute, Carlisle Barracks, PA)

Detachment 404 based in Ceylon sent teams from the Arakan Field Unit on missions to reconnoiter beaches and rivers on the Burmese coast. This OG team prepare to carry their rubber boats down to waiting British landing craft for an amphibious operation. (NARA)

Detachment 404 also dropped off agents on coastlines throughout the Indian Ocean, although P564 – an 85ft Air Sea Rescue launch – was limited by its short 500-mile range to infiltrating agents along the Burmese coast. (NARA)

source of information before it was crippled by the Japanese takeover from the Vichy French authorities in March 1945. The following month the SO "Gorilla" Team that had parachuted near a withdrawing French column was itself forced to retreat to the Chinese border after fighting its way out of a Japanese ambush. Attempts by the OSS to recruit French agents to infiltrate Indochina were frustrated by France's lack of cooperation. A viable alternative was found after the OSS received reports of skirmishes between the Japanese and the Viet Minh, the Communist underground movement led by Ho Chi Minh astride Vietnam's far northern border with China. In July 1945 the SO "Deer" Team parachuted in to train and supply the Viet Minh for sabotage operations. Christened the "Bo Doi Viet-My" (Vietnamese-American Unit), it was still training when news of the Japanese surrender arrived on 15 August 1945. Meanwhile the "Quail" Team, a POW Mercy Mission with OSS personnel, landed at Hanoi's Gia Lam airport and evacuated Allied POWs without incident.

The Pacific

Although the OSS was not allowed to operate in the Pacific Theater, Adm Nimitz did accept the transfer of an MU Operational Swimmer Group to help form UDT-10 in Hawaii in June 1944. The US Navy created UDTs after

E **MARITIME UNIT**
1 & 2: LAMBERTSEN AMPHIBIOUS RESPIRATORY UNIT

Early and later models of the LARU, a self-contained underwater "rebreather" device designed to allow swimmers to conduct maritime sabotage undetected. The early model (1) was sent to an MU swimmer unit in Britain, but technical problems and the lack of a clear mission prevented it from being used in Europe. The later model (2) had its components contained in canvas; another MU swimmer unit in Ceylon tested it, but the war ended before it could be deployed operationally.

3: UNDERWATER DEMOLITION TEAM 10; CENTRAL PACIFIC, SUMMER 1944

Although no longer part of the OSS, most of the personnel of UDT-10 were swimmers from the Maritime Unit. Their role was to survey landing beaches and demolish any obstacles that might hinder landing craft. This swimmer is preparing for a demolition mission, carrying a satchel charge containing C-2 plastic explosive. He is also holding the rubber swim fins that were introduced by MU swimmers and soon adopted by all UDTs.

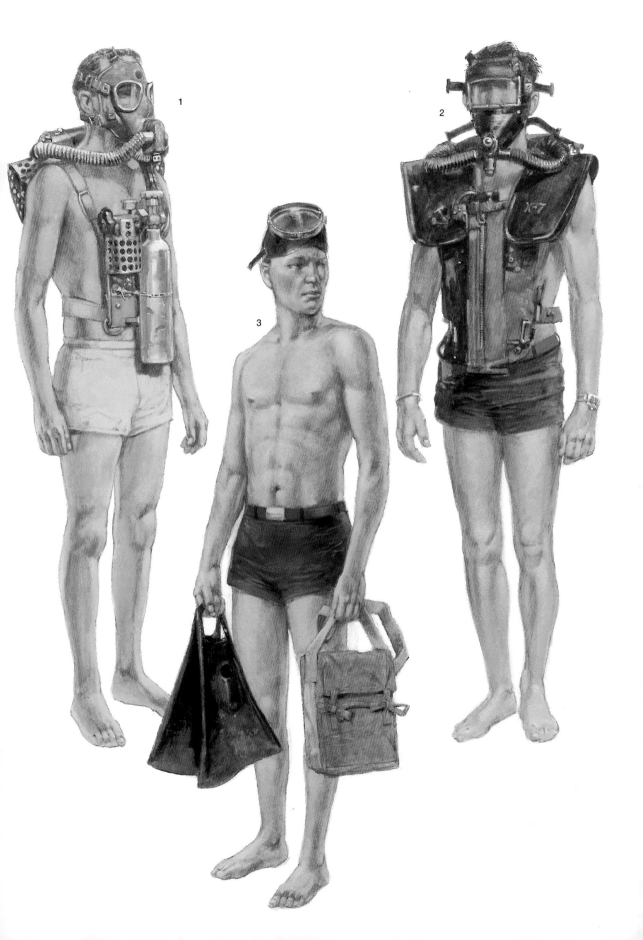

Members of the SO "Deer" Team stand in formation in front of the Viet Minh they have been training in French North Vietnam in August 1945. Although news of the Japanese surrender arrived before the "Deer" Team could lead them into action, the Viet Minh attacked the Japanese garrison at Thai Nguyen on August 20, 1945 as they marched on Hanoi to declare an independent Vietnam. (Courtesy René Defourneaux)

the heavy casualties suffered at Tarawa, where reefs and shallow water forced Marines to wade ashore under fire. UDTs were trained to scout the approaches to landing beaches, demolish any natural or man-made obstacles, and help guide landing craft to the beach. UDT-10's first assignment became the only UDT mission launched from a submarine during the war, when a five-man team was assigned to the USS *Burrfish* to scout the Yap and Palau Islands in August 1944; three men did not return from a nighttime reconnaissance of Gagil Tomil, and their fate remains uncertain. The rest of UDT-10 operated from the transport USS *Ratheburne* when they surveyed beaches and demolished coral for the landings at Anguar and Ulithi Atoll in September 1944. UDT-10's last wartime missions were scouting landing beaches at Leyte in October 1944 and Luzon in January 1945.

CHINA
Sino-American Cooperative Organization
The exclusion of the OSS from the Pacific Theater made Donovan look to China as the best opportunity for operations against Japan. Tai Li, who headed the Chinese intelligence service BIS, did not want an American service functioning in China outside his control. He was amicable with Capt Milton Miles, leader of the US Naval Group China that reported on Japanese coastal shipping and the weather in support of US Navy operations in the Pacific. Miles believed that absolute cooperation with Tai Li was the only way to operate successfully in China, so, anxious to establish itself in-country, the OSS joined with Tai Li and Miles to form SACO in April 1943, with Tai Li as its director and Miles as his deputy. Miles also doubled as the head of both the US Naval Group and the OSS in China. The OSS provided supplies and instructors to SACO, but its plans to gather intelligence independently were thwarted by Tai Li, who wished to conceal China's actual internal situation from the Americans. Miles, who did not want the mission of the Naval Group jeopardized by another organization that he directed, was unhelpful, and Donovan personally fired him from the OSS in Chungking in December 1943. Although OSS personnel served in SACO for the rest of the war, Donovan believed the OSS would have more freedom of action by joining forces with another American unit in China, the US Army Fourteenth Air Force.

Air and Ground Forces Resources and Technical Staff
Gen Claire Chennault's legendary status in China as the founder of the "Flying Tigers" was beyond reproach, even by Tai Li. In April 1944

AGFRTS was formed with staff from both the OSS and Chennault's Fourteenth Air Force. AGFRTS allowed the OSS to gather intelligence independently, and to help Chennault employ his limited air assets effectively. In April 1944 the Japanese launched a series of offensives in central and southern China to seize USAAF bases and a secure land route between Beijing and French Indochina. With Nationalist Chinese forces routed, AGFRTS teams conducted a sabotage and ambush campaign in an attempt to slow the Japanese advance, and were forced to demolish several

ABOVE The "Deer" Team's Lt René Defourneaux (standng, second from left), with Viet Minh leader Ho Chi Minh (third from left), team leader Maj Allison Thomas (center), and Vo Nguyen Giap (in suit and tie), the future commanding general in the Communists' wars against both the French and the US-backed Republic of Vietnam between 1948 and 1975. Contrary to popular belief, although medic Paul Hoagland (far right) treated Ho for malaria, dengue fever and dysentery he did not save his life. (Courtesy René Defourneaux)

LEFT Lt Raymond Hairston (far left) of the SO "Camel" Team operated in eastern China with Chinese guerrillas for more than four months in early 1945. They ambushed convoys, gathered intelligence, and collected Japanese small arms to sustain the guerrillas. See Plate C1. (Courtesy Ron Hairston)

SO teams worked with Chinese guerrillas as far as 500 miles behind Japanese lines, mostly being parachuted in; some SO personnel in China had already seen action in France. One unexpected challenge faced by OG instructors sent in to train the first Chinese paratroop units was that they were provided with Chinese soldiers who lacked basic training or did not meet the physical requirements. The Americans' efforts rectified these problems and made the Chinese Commandos an effective fighting force in the closing days of the war. (Pete Lutken Collection, ARSOF Archives, JFK Special Warfare Museum)

USAAF bases before they could be captured. AGFRTS was fully absorbed into the OSS in April 1945.

The "Dixie" Mission

In July 1944 OSS personnel participated in a mission to Yenan to liaise with the Communist Chinese and assess their potential. They provided the mission with a communication link with Chungking, supplied the Communists with radio equipment, demonstrated demolition techniques, and joined the Communists as observers on operations behind Japanese lines. The Communists provided information on Japanese units and allowed the OSS to microfilm their collection of Japanese documents and newspapers. Not all these interactions went smoothly. The OSS wanted to use Yenan as a base to infiltrate SI teams into northern China, Manchuria and Korea, and also to

 DETACHMENT 101

1: NORTHERN BURMA, FALL 1943

Detachment 101 set up several bases behind Japanese lines, and the only reliable method of transportation between them or out of Burma entirely was on foot. OSS personnel in the jungle did not adhere to uniform standards, and wore whatever was practical. This bearded operative is wearing a herringbone twill field cap, khaki uniform and Type III service shoes. His M36 pistol belt, M1916 holster, M1912 clip pouch and compass case are standard issue, and he carries the M1 carbine.

2: KACHIN GUERRILLA; NORTHERN BURMA, FALL 1943

Unlike the other native peoples of Burma, the Kachins fought the Japanese out of pure conviction to drive out their occupiers. Before they were issued with US military clothing they fought in their native garb, always with their *dah*

shortswords strapped across their chests. This Kachin's main weapon is a British SMLE rifle – easy to procure from British stocks in India – but fitted with a sling normally used for Thompson submachine guns.

3: EASTERN BURMA, SPRING 1945

This operative is better equipped for jungle warfare, with M1943 pattern herringbone twill shirt and trousers (showing differential fading of older and newer issue items) and a British bush hat. His canvas jungle boots with rubber soles were popular for their quick-drying qualities in the constantly wet jungle. He is armed with a silenced M3 "grease gun," with the special HiStandard barrel designed for the muffled elimination of enemy personnel. People who fired it liked it; the silenced barrel weighed down the muzzle, which in the standard M3 tended to climb from the recoil of firing.

OG instructors use a derelict C-47 fuselage to demonstrate the proper jump procedure to future Chinese Commandos. (NARA)

arm and train the Communists for sabotage operations against the Japanese. These plans were shelved after the Communists demanded a $20 million loan (which was the total amount of unvouchered funds budgeted to the OSS in 1944). However, the Dixie Mission in one form or another remained in Yenan until March 1947.

In May 1945 the SO "Spaniel" Team parachuted into northern China to enlist Chinese for intelligence and sabotage operations, but were detained by the Communists, who had not been informed in advance. The Communists wanted to maintain their monopoly of providing intelligence, and to prevent any independent contacts that might reveal – contrary to their propaganda – their fairly tranquil coexistence with the Japanese. The Spaniel Team was held incommunicado until the end of the war.

Independent operations

In February 1945 the new CBI theater commander, Gen Wedemeyer, ordered the OSS to be made an independent command as Detachment 202, in charge of all American clandestine operations in China. This allowed SI to set up independent networks in southern China. The Japanese did not occupy large rural areas but kept their garrisons in the towns, and SO teams exploited this when leading Chinese guerrillas on a sustained campaign of sabotage and ambush. In April 1945 OG personnel started training the Chinese Commando units that became their country's first paratroopers, and in July, accompanied by their OG advisors, the Commandos supported a Nationalist Chinese offensive in southern China. Deployed by parachute or sampan, they disrupted river and road traffic and helped seize an airfield. Two other Commando units served as the honor guard for the surrender talks at Nanking in August 1945.

Mercy Missions

With the sudden end of the war in early August 1945 the safety of thousands of POWs in Japanese hands became an immediate concern. Since known POW camps in China were hundreds of miles from Allied territory an approach by air was the only way to get to them quickly. The OSS established Mercy Missions with the Air Ground Aid Service that was responsible for rescuing downed airmen and POWs; these missions parachuted near POW camps throughout China, along with Nissei interpreters and medical supplies. The Japanese units they encountered were initially unaware the war was over, but cooperated fully once they were officially informed by their superiors. The missions reported on the condition of the POWs, provided medical attention, and began to facilitate their evacuation. At a camp at Mukden in Manchuria the "Cardinal" Team found Gen Jonathan Wainwright, who in May 1942 had surrendered the Philippines; the general was evacuated in time to participate in the surrender ceremonies on the USS *Missouri* in Tokyo Bay on 2 September 1945.

WEAPONS & EQUIPMENT

R&D helped develop special weapons and equipment for the OSS, but most of them either never left the drawingboard, never progressed beyond prototypes, or never found a use in the field. For reasons of space, only those that saw use with the OSS will be mentioned here.[1]

Special weapons

The OSS issued its own variant of the Sykes-Fairbairn knife, with a thinner blade than that issued to the British Commandos. While this made it very effective for slashing and stabbing the tip of the brittle blade often broke. One OSS veteran only saw them being used to open ration cans; others believed that the standard issue M3 trench knife was more practical for the field.

The United Defense Model 42 (UD-42) 9mm submachine gun, known as the Marlin after the company subcontracted to manufacture it, was initially produced for the Dutch East Indies forces, but the OSS took over the contract when those colonies fell to the Japanese in 1942. They used it worldwide, and supplied significant quantities to resistance forces. Able to fire at 750rpm, it was noted by OG teams as being handy at close range; two 20-round magazines were clipped together in staggered fashion for fast reloading.

With its suppressed discharge and lack of muzzle flash, the ten-shot HiStandard .22cal silenced pistol was ideal for eliminating enemy personnel at close range virtually undetected. Its built-in "silencer" reduced the sound of discharge by 90 percent, and out of doors the remaining report (similar to snapping fingers) could easily be smothered by everyday background noise. HiStandard also produced a special barrel for the M3 "grease gun" SMG that also reduced the sound of discharge by 90 percent; this saw action with Detachment 101 in Burma and SO teams in China.

The Liberator pistol did not originate with the OSS but from the Military Intelligence Service at the War Department. Cheaply made out of seamless tubing and stamped sheet metal, the Liberator was an extremely crude single-shot .45cal smooth-bore pistol with an effective range of only 10ft. It was

---

[1] For a more extensive account see Dr John W. Brunner's *OSS Weapons II*, listed in the Select Bibliography.

A member of the SO "Chicago" Mission leans on a pile of UD-42 Marlin submachine guns to be distributed to Communist Greek partisans in 1944. The "Chicago" personnel spent more time behind enemy lines than any other OSS team in Greece. (Courtesy Patrick K. O'Donnell)

shipped in great numbers to Europe and the Southwest Pacific, where it did see action in the Philippines. Plans to drop Liberators to resistance groups in Europe were shelved because of fears that spreading thousands of these un-numbered weapons across the countryside would pose a serious postwar criminal problem. The OSS received a large number of Liberators, but neither OSS personnel nor guerrilla groups were interested in them since vastly more reliable weapons, either Allied-supplied or Axis captures, were readily available. Most of the Liberators that found their way to OSS personnel were kept simply as souvenirs.

Standard issue weapons
Many OSS personnel who served overseas neither used nor encountered any of the silencers or other special weapons that were developed with them in

G VARIOUS BRANCHES
1: RESEARCH & DEVELOPMENT
This engineer is preparing to test-fire the "Big Joe 5" crossbow, designed to silently take out sentries and guard dogs. Heavy-duty rubber bands under tension would propel an aluminum dart to a range of 80 yards or an incendiary flare up to 200 yards. Developed under contract by Northwestern University, the Big Joe 5, like the other crossbows designed for the OSS, was never shot in anger. Other specialized inventions that did not see action include the Beano grenade, spigot mortar, Stinger, and exploding flour.

2: FIELD PHOTOGRAPHIC
The Field Photographic Unit used a wide variety of still and motion picture cameras, including this Mitchell. Many of its personnel were Hollywood cameramen and technicians who had worked for director John Ford, who established and led Field Photo during the war. Naval dress was the predominant uniform for this unit, and this officer is wearing a B-1 summer flying cap and G-1 leather flying jacket.

3: RESEARCH & ANALYSIS
One of the strongest assets of the OSS was its small army of researchers and analysts, who evaluated and produced reports based on the intelligence gathered by agents overseas. Many of the documents sent to R&A Headquarters in Washington arrived in the form of microfilm so as to save on cargo space in transit. This analyst is using a Recordak Model C microfilm reader, which accepted both 16mm and 35mm film and was specifically designed to view microfilmed copies of newspapers, mechanical drawings and diagrams.

mind. They were armed with standard weapons, and often just a pistol. This included SI agents, whose primary job was to gather intelligence while avoiding direct contact with the enemy; they carried pistols for self-defense, but these were incriminating if discovered. The most common of a wide variety employed by OSS personnel were the Colt M1903 and M1911A1 semiautomatics; the former's compact size made it suitable for concealment in a pocket.

Both the fixed-stock M1 carbine and folding-stock M1A1 were common issue in the OSS; M1 Garand rifles were mostly issued to Operational Groups, but a few Jedburghs did trade their carbines for the Garand's greater stopping power. The sniper variant of the M1903A4 Springfield, with the Weaver telescopic sight, saw use in Burma and China. The OSS supplemented its Marlin SMGs with Thompsons, M3s and Stens. Light machine guns employed included the Bren, Browning Automatic Rifle, and the M1919 .30cal air-cooled machine gun.

The OSS employed both the M1 and M9 versions of the bazooka in convoy ambushes. Mortars were also used; Jedburgh teams supplied easily portable British 2in mortars to the Maquis, and higher caliber models including the M2 60mm, M1 81mm and the 4.2in were also used by SO and OG teams. When faced with situations that required heavier fire support, the OG "Louise" Team in southern France had four M3 37mm antitank guns dropped to them in August 1944. Only two of them functioned, and were used to shell German-occupied Vallon; a counterattack forced Louise to abandon them after a fierce fight.

Grenades were standard issue to OSS teams in the field, and were also supplied in ample numbers to the resistance. British No.82 "Gammon" grenades were reported by one SO operative in France to be able to knock out any type of vehicle. Kachin guerrillas would connect anything from 25 to as many as 100 Mk II fragmentation grenades with primacord and place them along jungle trails, producing a murderous gauntlet for any unwary Japanese patrol.

Sabotage[2]

Many of the sabotage devices employed were improved versions of originally British inventions. Composition C was the primary explosive used by the OSS against infrastructure targets, in designations C-1 through C-3 indicating different combinations of explosive and plasticizing ingredients. The Limpet was designed for maritime sabotage; a waterproof plastic case holding 2.5lbs of Torpex could be attached to a steel hull with six Alnico magnets. A variant called the Pin-Up Girl used a pin-firing device instead of magnets to secure itself to a wooden hull. Used on land, the Clam was a plastic case holding a ½lb plastic charge that could be attached to any metal surface with four magnets.

The firing devices used by the OSS to initiate explosions were (with three exceptions) of British origin, and relied upon a timing device, the pulling out of a pin, pressure, or pressure-release. The US-designed Mole was intended to derail entire trains inside tunnels; its photo-cell eye, normally exposed to daylight, would trigger an explosion when blacked out by the train entering the tunnel. Another sophisticated US device was the Anerometer, a 6in cylinder attached to a short fabric tube of plastic explosive. Designed to destroy aircraft in flight, it was initiated by a drop in external atmospheric pressure, normally at 1,500ft after takeoff.

The Pocket Incendiary was designed to spontaneously combust after a time delay; containing napalm powder and several acids, it would burn by itself for 8–12 minutes after ignition of a celluloid capsule of potassium chlorate by two Signal Relay Incendiary Pencils using regular match-heads. The Firefly was an incendiary device small enough to slip into a vehicle's gas tank or a fuel drum; small holes admitted gasoline, causing two rubber washers to swell, which triggered a small amount of TNT and magnesium.

Communications

To allow OSS agents to transmit intelligence while operating undercover, in late 1942 the Communications branch developed the Special Services Transmitter Receiver Model No.1 (SSTR-1). This had three components – a transmitter, a receiver, and a power supply – that were all compact enough to fit together in a small suitcase. Various power supply units gave a total weight range of from 20lb to 44lb. The SSTR-1 had a transmission range from 300 to 1,000 miles, and messages were tapped out with a telegraph key on a continuous wave; it used interchangeable crystals that allowed it to operate on different frequencies. Unfortunately the SSTR-1 was fragile, and many were damaged during parachute drops. Its power pack proved troublesome due to poor connections, shorts, insufficient insulation and overheating. The 6-volt battery that powered it had a short life, but could be recharged in the field with portable thermocouple chargers that burned wood or gasoline. The SSTR-1 itself could be powered by a hand-cranked generator, car batteries, or from the electrical current of a building. OSS agents also used SOE communication equipment including the Type 3 Mk II and Type A Mk III

---

[2] For fuller technical information on explosives and firing devices, see Elite 160: *World War II Infantry Assault Tactics*, and also Elite 100: *World War II Axis Booby Traps & Sabotage Tactics*.

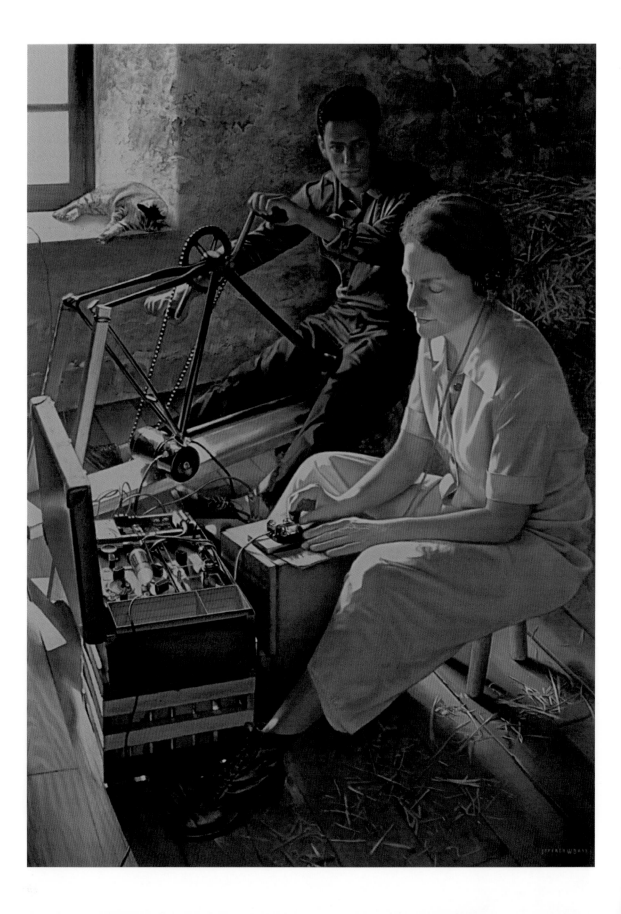

suitcase radios; these weighed 32lb and 39lb respectively and had a transmission range of at least 500 miles.

OSS agents who transmitted while undercover always risked being located by German radio detection equipment, often operated in mobile vans, and the Joan-Eleanor (J-E) system was invented in response. J-E came in two components: Joan was an SSTC-502 transceiver powered by two 1.5-volt and two 67.5-volt batteries; its signals could be received by an orbiting plane from 30 miles away and, weighing only 3½lb, its small size made it ideal for undercover work. Joan worked best in clear, open surroundings. Its counterpart was Eleanor, a 40lb unit consisting of an SSTR-6 transceiver, wire recorder, antenna extension support, manual directional control, dynamotor, and a power supply containing four 6-volt wet cell batteries. Mounted aboard an aircraft, Eleanor could record 60 minutes of transmissions verbatim on a spool of wire. Eleanor was located in the bomb bay of several British-supplied USAAF Mosquito PR XVIs; at 30,000ft, Eleanor had to be turned on every half-hour to keep it from freezing. J-E's narrow UHF beam made detection impossible and codes unnecessary. J-E proved successful when it was first used in occupied Holland in November 1944, and was supplied to several teams that parachuted into Germany in 1945. The Eleanor operator and the agent were able to talk with each other from 10–30 miles away, and clarify any details being reported. Special broadcasts by the BBC were used to schedule these rendezvous between the agent and the circling Mosquito.

The OSS also used standard US Army Signal Corps radios for field operations. The 35lb SCR-300 was a backpack radio that transmitted voice messages over ranges of 3–5 miles. The SCR-694 could transmit voice and coded messages with a transmission range of 15–30 miles; it weighed nearly 200lbs, but could be broken down and carried in several components, and SO teams in China powered it with the GN-58 hand-cranked generator. For small unit actions, SO and OG teams used the SCR-536 "handi-talkie" with its 1-mile transmission range. Each SF Detachment was equipped with three jeep-mounted SCR-193 radios and a truck-mounted SCR-399. The SCR-193, with a range of 15–60 miles, would maintain contact between liaison officers in the field and the SCR-399 at army headquarters; the SCR-399, with a range of 100–250 miles, would pass and receive messages to and from SFHQ in London.

Ciphers

Although "code" is the term generically used, "code" and "cipher" are distinct. Codes have entire words replaced by other words, letters, numbers or symbols. Ciphers have individual letters in messages replaced by other letters.

OSS agents initially coded their messages with a double transposition system. The agent would select a specific line from a poem, song or book; this would identify a transmission's origin and become the agent's base cipher when preparing messages. For security reasons, only the agent and the headquarters that received the messages knew what the line was. This system proved to be too time-consuming and vulnerable to garbled radio traffic and human error. It was soon replaced by one of the most unbreakable ciphers ever devised: the one-time pad.

Invented after World War I, this was first supplied by the SOE before the OSS provided its own version. The OTP is a polyalphabetic cipher where any letter in the alphabet can be substituted for any letter in a message without a

OPPOSITE Painting commissioned by Richard J. Guggenhime, showing SO agent Virginia Hall tapping out a message to London with a British SOE Type 3 Mk II suitcase radio, while French resistance leader Edmond Lebrat provides power with an improvised hand-cranked generator. Hall reported on German troop movements, and directed 400 Maquis fighters who ambushed convoys and sabotaged rail lines; she became the first civilian woman to be awarded the Distinguished Service Cross. This painting by Jeff Bass currently hangs at CIA Headquarters. (Courtesy Jeff Bass)

Since Detachment 101 was at the end of a very long supply chain they relied on local resources to sustain operations, which included scratch-building their own radios. Scrapyards and junkpiles were searched for parts, while the wooden housings were made from shipping crates. These 23lb custom-built radios were powered by dry cell batteries and had an effective range of 800 to 1,200 miles. (William J. Donovan Collection, US Army Military History Institute, Carlisle Barracks, PA)

set key or pattern. The letters on the OTP to code the message were completely random, so two identical letters in one plain text message would have a different cipher letter. The OTP was a tablet of 100 sheets of nitrate rice paper that could easily be burned, dissolved or eaten. Each sheet was glued on top of the next so that only one could be used at a time. Rows of random letters in sets of five were printed on each sheet. The letters of the plain text message would be written under the letters on the OTP. Next, a table of letters printed on a silk handkerchief was used to obtain the needed cipher letters; the cipher letters used in the transmission were where the plain text and the OTP letters intersected on the table. This process was reversed when an OTP message was deciphered. The agent and headquarters required the exact OTP for this ciphering system to work. Each sheet could only be used once, and each following sheet would provide a coded message dissimilar from the previous one. This meant that if an OTP and its conversion table fell into enemy hands it still could not be used to break other OTP messages because of the randomness of its letters.

Undercover: clothing, documents, accessories

The OSS bought, scrounged or made civilian clothing for its agents sent into occupied territory. Continental styles were noticeably different from American or British fashions. The OSS at first obtained suits, overcoats, hats, shoes and other items from European refugees and second-hand shops, but since these only offered a limited supply authentic copies were tailor-made, perfect down to the parallel threading of the buttons. Towards the end of the war the OSS faced a shortage of German-style clothing, so one OSS supply officer followed American troops into Cologne and collected clothing and personal items from abandoned shops before anyone else could loot them. The OSS also obtained German uniforms from POW camps or captured stocks; these were mostly worn by German and Austrian agents who went behind the lines to gather intelligence or spread MO material – one female agent parachuted behind the lines dressed as a German Army nurse. Before going on these missions, some agents actually infiltrated POW camps in German uniforms to gather intelligence and to learn the current colloquial style and mannerisms of German soldiers.

The most important thing an agent carried were identity papers and any occupation permits necessary to operate freely. For instance, in France an OSS agent needed an identity card, ration cards (for food, clothing and tobacco), census card, occupation card, certificate of residence, medical certificate (to excuse the agent from labor or military service), work permit and birth certificate. Agents operating in Germany required additional papers such as travel permits and police registrations for employment and housing. Depending on an agent's cover, a foreign worker passport or a Wehrmacht pay book would also be issued. R&D forged most of these documents from

In the radio hut at Detachment 404 HQ in Ceylon radio operators wait to receive transmissions from agents in the field. The OSS employed a wide variety of radios, including the civilian RCA receivers seen here. Note the paperback novel beyond the typewriter (center); agents had to memorize a particular line from a specific book to use as the base code when encrypting messages for transmission back to base. (NARA)

1

2

3

3° CONTINGENT O.C

4

5

6

7

8

9

10

11

As Allied armies advanced up Italy in 1944, OG teams were parachuted into the northern half of the country to work with partisan groups against the Germans. Note at right the "Special Recon Bn" sleeve title above the Fifth Army patch on this man's tank jacket – see Plate H2. (NARA)

H INSIGNIA

1: SPECIAL FORCE JUMP WINGS
Issued to Jedburgh teams, these were designed by the British Capt Victor Andrew Gough, a "Jed" who was later captured and executed by the Germans. Operational Groups and Special Operations teams that deployed from Britain also wore them.

2: SPECIAL RECON BATTALION SLEEVE TITLE
Worn by Operational Groups in the Mediterranean that became part of the 2671st Special Reconnaissance Battalion (Provisional).

3: CONTINGENT OPERATIONAL GROUP PATCH
Created by OG personnel who conducted operations from the Yugoslavian island of Vis, its design was based on that of the British Combined Operations patch. Some OG personnel in Greece also wore it.

DETACHMENT 101 PATCHES:
4: USA KACHIN RANGERS PATCH
5: USA JINGPAW RANGERS PATCH
6: LATER JINGPAW RANGERS PATCH
4 & 5 were originally made for Detachment 101 but were never officially issued, due to concerns that the "USA" might be provocative to the British who provided the great majority of Allied forces in Burma; they also looked too similar to the CBI patch. **6** was the subsequent altered version.

7: DETACHMENT 101 BURMA CAMPAIGN BAR
Awarded to the Kachins for their service with Detachment 101.

8: CITATION FOR MILITARY ASSISTANCE MEDAL
Erroneously manufactured and awarded to the Kachins as the result of a mistake made by a radio operator receiving a supply request. He misunderstood "CMA" in the message to mean "Citation for Military Assistance Medal" instead of "comma."

9: CHINA IDENTIFICATION BADGE
Issued to American and Chinese OSS agents who operated in the field in 1945.

10: OSS VETERAN PIN
Issued by Gen Donovan, along with a certificate, to those who had served in the OSS, after it was disbanded in October 1945.

11: CHINESE 1st WAR AREA MARAUDER CORPS BADGE
Issued to American and Chinese OSS agents who operated in eastern China. It was provided along with the China identification badge.

genuine examples collected by undercover agents; German papers were gathered in captured towns, POW camps, and from dead enemy soldiers. German typewriters, stamps, watermarks, ink, and blank cards and permits were highly sought-after by R&D personnel, since genuine documents that were simply filled out withstood greater scrutiny than those fabricated from scratch. Some documents were difficult to forge, such as German ration cards that were valid for only four weeks at a time. Recently bombed cities or areas were listed as the agent's place of birth or current residence to make background checks of his cover story difficult. Any mistake could doom an agent; one was caught when his work permit was found to have been signed supposedly in two different cities with the same handwriting.

The simplest things carried in agents' pockets could support or jeopardize their cover stories. Before they left for the field they were searched for such obvious items as London theater-ticket stubs. One agent maintained his cover in France by carrying Lotterie Nationale tickets and a letter sent to his Paris address that he had someone write for him. Another agent infiltrating Rome even lined his pockets with Italian tobacco shavings.

Cameras were issued to OSS agents, the Minox miniature camera being the most ideal. Manufactured in Latvia, the Minox remained scarce despite a nationwide search by the OSS. To make up for the shortage the OSS developed its own miniature Matchbox camera (this came with German, Swedish and Japanese labels to make it look like a simple box of matches, hence its name). It could take 34 pictures on 16mm film, but could only be reloaded in the dark. Agents knew that a camera would be incriminating if discovered during a search, so many either did quick sketches of important targets or just committed them to memory.

In the event of capture, OSS agents were supplied with the rubber-coated potassium cyanide "L" (for lethal) pill for a quick suicide. One female agent used one in 1945 after being shot by a German patrol while attempting to cross into Switzerland from Germany.

Maritime equipment

Invented by Dr Christian Lambertsen, the **Lambertsen Amphibious Respiratory Unit** (see Plate E) was adopted by the OSS after it was demonstrated to them in a swimming pool in November 1942; the LARU came in four different models, weighing 28–35lb. This self-contained apparatus allowed a diver to stay undetected for several hours underwater at depths of 50–100ft by preventing any telltale bubbles escaping. Pure oxygen at a pressure of 2,000lb per square inch flowed from a cylinder attached to the diver's chest into his face piece and a rubber "lung" on his back. The exhaled air went through a canister of lime above the lung that absorbed the carbon dioxide before being breathed again by the diver. Divers had to discipline themselves to breathe slowly and evenly for the CO_2 to be completely absorbed; breathing too quickly overloaded the LARU and caused discomfort. The diver was also supplied with oxygen from the lung, which was replenished from the cylinder when necessary. The LARU proved its worth in July 1944, when Operational Swimmer Group 2 used them to swim undetected through the antisubmarine nets at Guantanamo Bay, Cuba. Despite this success, the LARU was never employed on missions against the enemy.

The **surfboard** was a pneumatic rubber floatation device that could be inflated in minutes with a compressed air cylinder. It was 10ft 6in long, 3ft wide and weighed 310lb, and could carry two men and their equipment to a

total of 900lb. It was propelled by a silent electric motor at 5 knots with a range of 15 miles. It was successfully used by the MU on the Adriatic coast of Italy in the summer of 1944. The MU also employed a two-man **kayak** for coastal operations; this had a plywood frame fitted together with metal pipe and covered in rubberized canvas, and was propelled by two collapsible double-bladed paddles. Carried in two backpacks weighing 50lb each, the 16ft 6in kayak could be assembled in five to ten minutes, weighed 104lb and had a carrying capacity of 800lb. It was widely used by MU teams for reconnaissance along the Burmese coast in early 1945.

TRANSPORTATION

Royal Air Force Special Duty squadrons based in Britain and the Mediterranean to support SIS and SOE operations also dropped OSS agents into Europe. A Halifax parachuted the first OSS agents into France in June 1943 and Germany in September 1944. SD squadrons of Halifaxes and Stirlings also dropped Jedburgh and OG teams, while Lysanders landed OSS agents individually in France. In the Far East, RAF Liberators, Dakotas and Catalinas supported OSS operations in Burma and Thailand.

In November 1943 the USAAF established the 801st Bombardment Group (redesignated 492nd BG in August 1944) with B-24 Liberator squadrons that had previously flown patrols against U-boats; their long-distance night flying experience made these aircrews ideal for supporting clandestine operations in Europe. Nicknamed the "Carpetbaggers," they flew their first missions in January 1944 from Tempsford, and later from Harrington. Each glossy black B-24 was specially modified to drop up to eight agents and 12 supply containers. After September 1944, with most of Northwest Europe liberated, a few Carpetbagger squadrons were transferred to Italy, while other Carpetbagger B-24s had their armament removed to fly supplies into Sweden for the Sepals. Supply missions were also flown for the resistance in Norway and Denmark. Due to the strong anti-aircraft defenses over Germany the slow B-24s only flew over the southwest corner of the Reich, while faster A-26 Invaders were used to drop OSS agents over the rest of Germany. The agent in the A-26 would sit on a hinged plywood floor in the bomb bay; once over the drop zone the agent would fall out when the floor folded from beneath him. The last Carpetbagger mission was flown in April 1945.

Along with Royal Navy MTBs and Italian MAS boats, US Navy Patrol Torpedo boats of RON 15 landed OSS agents throughout the western Mediterranean from 1943 to 1944. RON 2 (2), based at Dartmouth on the

"Carpetbagger" missions from Harrington airfield north of London were flown at low level and only during a full moon, so that the ground could be seen. The glossy black Liberators dropped their agents from 400–600ft at just above stalling speed. Under magnification this B-24 can be seen to have flame dampers attached to the muzzles of the machine guns in the top turret. Note that the ventral ball turret has been removed; agents parachuted from the resulting "Joe hole." (NARA)

PT 199 was a 78ft Higgins boat that operated with PT 71 and PT 72 in RON 2 (2) in the English Channel during the spring of 1944. Each boat was armed with a 37mm cannon on the bow, twin .50cal machine guns port and starboard and a 20mm cannon mounted aft. The torpedo tubes were removed for greater speed and range. A modified Surfboat designed to land agents and supplies on enemy-held shores silently was provided to each PT boat in the squadron. (WWII PT Boats Museum and Archives)

English Channel, had three PT boats under the command of Cdr John D. Bulkeley; these landed and picked up OSS and other Allied agents along the French coast in the spring of 1944. The PT boats were painted a shade called "Mountbatten pink" that made them almost invisible in the dawn and dusk. All the operations of RON 2 (2) were accomplished successfully without ever coming into contact with the Germans.

SELECT BIBLIOGRAPHY

Bartholomew-Feis, Dixee R., *The OSS and Ho Chi Minh: Unexpected Allies in the war against Japan* (Lawrence, KS: University Press of Kansas, 2006)

Beavan, Colin, *Operation Jedburgh* (New York: Viking, 2006)

Brunner, John W., *OSS Weapons II* (Williamstown, NJ: Phillips Publications, 2005)

Corvo, Max, *The OSS in Italy, 1942–1945* (New York: Praeger, 1990)

Deschamps, Hélène, *Spyglass: An Autobiography* (New York: H. Holt, 1995)

Downs, Jim, *World War II: OSS Tragedy in Slovakia* (Oceanside, CA: Liefrinck, 2002)

Dunlop, Richard, *Behind Japanese Lines, with the OSS in Burma* (Chicago, IL: Rand McNally, 1979)

Dunlop, Richard, *Donovan, America's Master Spy* (Chicago, IL: Rand McNally, 1982)

Dwyer, John B., *Commandos from the Sea: The History of Amphibious*

Special Warfare in World War II and the Korean War (Boulder, CO: Paladin Press, 1998)

Ford, Kirk, *OSS and the Yugoslav Resistance, 1943–1945* (College Station: Texas A&M University Press, 1992)

Freeman, Gregory A., *The Forgotten 500: The untold story of the men who risked all for the greatest rescue mission of World War II* (New York: Nal Caliber, 2007)

Giannaris, John; Olson, McKinley C., *Yannis* (Tarrytown, NY: Pilgrimage, 1988)

Heimark, Bruce H., *The OSS Norwegian Special Operations Group in World War II* (Westport, CT: Praeger, 1994)

Katz, Barry, *Foreign Intelligence: Research and Analysis in the Office of Strategic Services, 1942–1945* (Cambridge, MA: Harvard University Press, 1989)

Laurie, Clayton D., *The Propaganda Warriors: America's Crusade against Nazi Germany* (Lawrence, KS: University Press of Kansas, 1996)

Lucas, Peter, *OSS in World War II Albania* (McFarland & Co, 2007)

Mattingly, Robert E., *Herringbone Cloak-GI Dagger, Marines of the OSS* (Washington: History and Museums Division Headquarters, U.S. Marine Corps, 1989)

McBride, Joseph, *Searching for John Ford: A Life* (New York: St. Martin's Press, 2001)

McIntosh, Elizabeth P., *Sisterhood of Spies: The Women of the OSS* (Annapolis, MD: Naval Institute Press, 1998)

McNaughton, James C., *Nissei Linguists: Japanese Americans in the Military Intelligence Service during WWII* (Washington: Department of the Army, 2006)

Mills, Francis B.; Brunner, John W., *OSS Special Operations in China* (Williamstown, NJ: Phillips Publications, 2002)

O'Donnell, Patrick K., *Operatives, Spies, and Saboteurs: The Unknown Story of the Men and Women of World War II's OSS* (New York: Free Press, 2004)

O'Donnell, Patrick K., *The Brenner Assignment: The Untold Story of the Most Daring Spy Mission of World War II* (Cambridge, MA: Da Capo Press, 2008)

Pearson, Judith, *The Wolves at the Door: The True Story of America's Greatest Female Spy* (Guilford, CT: Lyons Press, 2005)

Persico, Joseph E., *Piercing the Reich: The Penetration of Nazi Germany by American Secret Agents during World War II* (New York: Viking Press, 1979)

Persico, Joseph E. *Roosevelt's Secret War: FDR and World War II Espionage* (New York: Random House, 2001)

Reynolds, E. Bruce, *Thailand's Secret War: The Free Thai, OSS, and SOE during World War II* (New York: Cambridge University Press, 2005)

Roosevelt, Kermit, *The War Report of the OSS* (New York: Walker, 1976)

Roosevelt, Kermit, *The Overseas Targets* (New York: Walker, 1976)

Vaugham, Hal, *FDR's Twelve Apostles: The Spies who paved the way for the invasion of North Africa* (Guilford, CT: Lyons Press, 2006)

Yu, Maochun, *OSS in China* (New Haven: Yale University Press, 1996)

INDEX